MARVEL

ULTIMATE SPIDER-MAN VS THE SINISTER 6

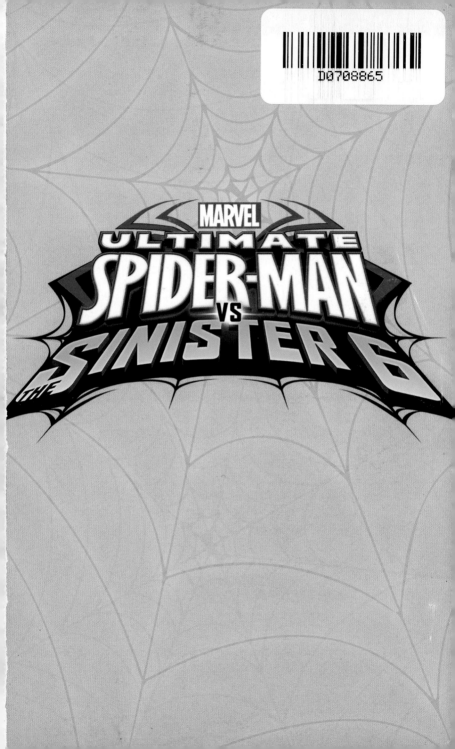

MARVEL UNIVERSE ULTIMATE SPIDER-MAN VS. THE SINISTER SIX VOL. 2. Contains material originally published in magazine form as MARVEL UNIVERSE ULTIMATE SPIDER-MAN VS. THE SINISTER SIX #5-8. First printing 2017. ISBN# 978-1-302-90259-9. Published by MARVEL WORLDWIDE, INC., a subsidiary of MARVEL ENTERTAINMENT, LLC. OFFICE OF PUBLICATION: 135 West 50th Street, New York, NY 10020. Copyright © 2017 MARVEL. No similarity between any of the names, characters, persons, and/or institutions in this magazine with those of any living or dead person or institution is intended, and any such similarity which may exist is purely coincidental. **Printed in the U.S.A.** DAN BUCKLEY, President, Marvel Entertainment; JOE QUESADA, Chief Creative Officer; TOM BREVOORT, SVP of Publishing; DAVID BOGART, SVP of Business Affairs & Operations, Publishing & Partnership; C.B. CEBULSKI, VP of Brand Management & Development, Asia; DAVID GABRIEL, SVP of Sales & Marketing, Publishing; JEFF YOUNGQUIST, VP of Production & Special Projects; DAN CARR, Executive Director of Publishing Technology; ALEX MORALES, Director of Publishing Operations; SUSAN CRESPI, Production Manager; STAN LEE, Chairman Emeritus. For information regarding advertising in Marvel Comics or on Marvel.com, please contact Vit DeBellis, Integrated Sales Manager, at vdebellis@marvel.com. For Marvel subscription inquiries, please call 888-511-5480. **Manufactured between 2/24/2017 and 3/28/2017 by SHERIDAN, CHELSEA, MI, USA.**

10 9 8 7 6 5 4 3 2 1

MARVEL
ULTIMATE
SPIDER-MAN
vs
THE SINISTER 6

BASED ON THE TV SERIES WRITTEN BY
KEVIN BURKE & CHRIS "DOC" WYATT AND JACOB SEMAHN

DIRECTED BY
YOUNG KI YOON, JAE WOO KIM & ROY BURDINE

ANIMATION PRODUCED BY
MARVEL ANIMATION STUDIOS WITH FILM ROMAN

ADAPTED BY
JOE CARAMAGNA

SPECIAL THANKS TO
HANNAH McDONALD & PRODUCT FACTORY

EDITORS
CHRISTINA HARRINGTON WITH MARK BASSO

SENIOR EDITOR
MARK PANICCIA

SPIDER-MAN CREATED BY **STAN LEE & STEVE DITKO**

Collection Editor: **Jennifer Grünwald**
Assistant Editor: **Caitlin O'Connell**
Associate Managing Editor: **Kateri Woody**
Editor, Special Projects: **Mark D. Beazley**
VP Production & Special Projects: **Jeff Youngquist**
SVP Print, Sales & Marketing: **David Gabriel**
Book Design: **Adam Del Re**

Head of Marvel Television: **Jeph Loeb**

Editor In Chief: **Axel Alonso**
Chief Creative Officer: **Joe Quesada**
President: **Dan Buckley**
Executive Producer: **Alan Fine**

ALONG CAME A SPIDER...
OR FIVE!

5: "LIZARDS"

WHILE ATTENDING A RADIOLOGY DEMONSTRATION, HIGH SCHOOL STUDENT PETER PARKER WAS BITTEN BY A RADIOACTIVE SPIDER AND GAINED THE SPIDER'S POWERS! NOW HE IS TRAINING WITH THE SUPERSPY ORGANIZATION CALLED S.H.I.E.L.D. TO BECOME THE...

MARVEL

ULTIMATE SPIDER-MAN VS THE SINISTER 6

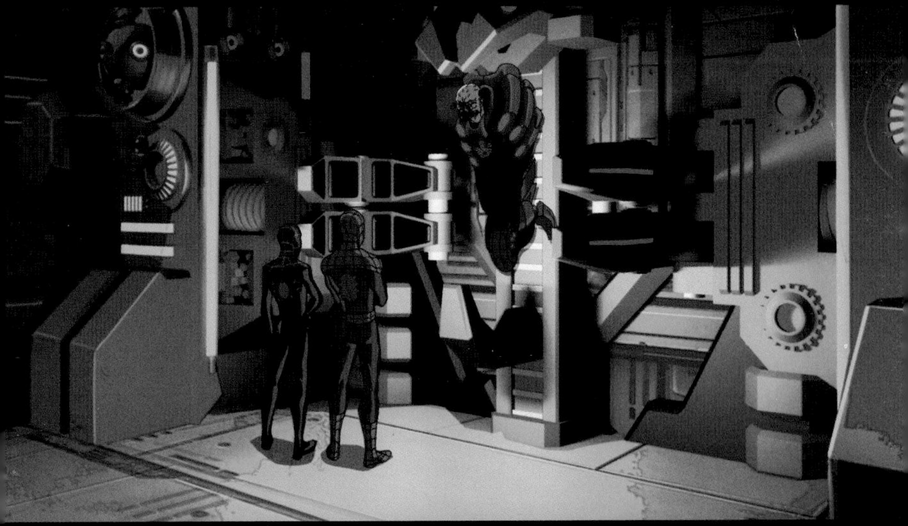

Sometimes one negative can trump a dozen positives. Things should be great–Spider-Man has a cool new job as a S.H.I.E.L.D. student-instructor, and when Doctor Octopus and Hydra teamed up to take over Nick Fury's little secret spy organization, the Web-Warriors kicked his metal cephalopod butt.

What's got Spidey down is he's learned that someone at S.H.I.E.L.D. is a spy for Doc Ock, and our spider-pals have to smoke him out before Hydra can finish the job they've started.

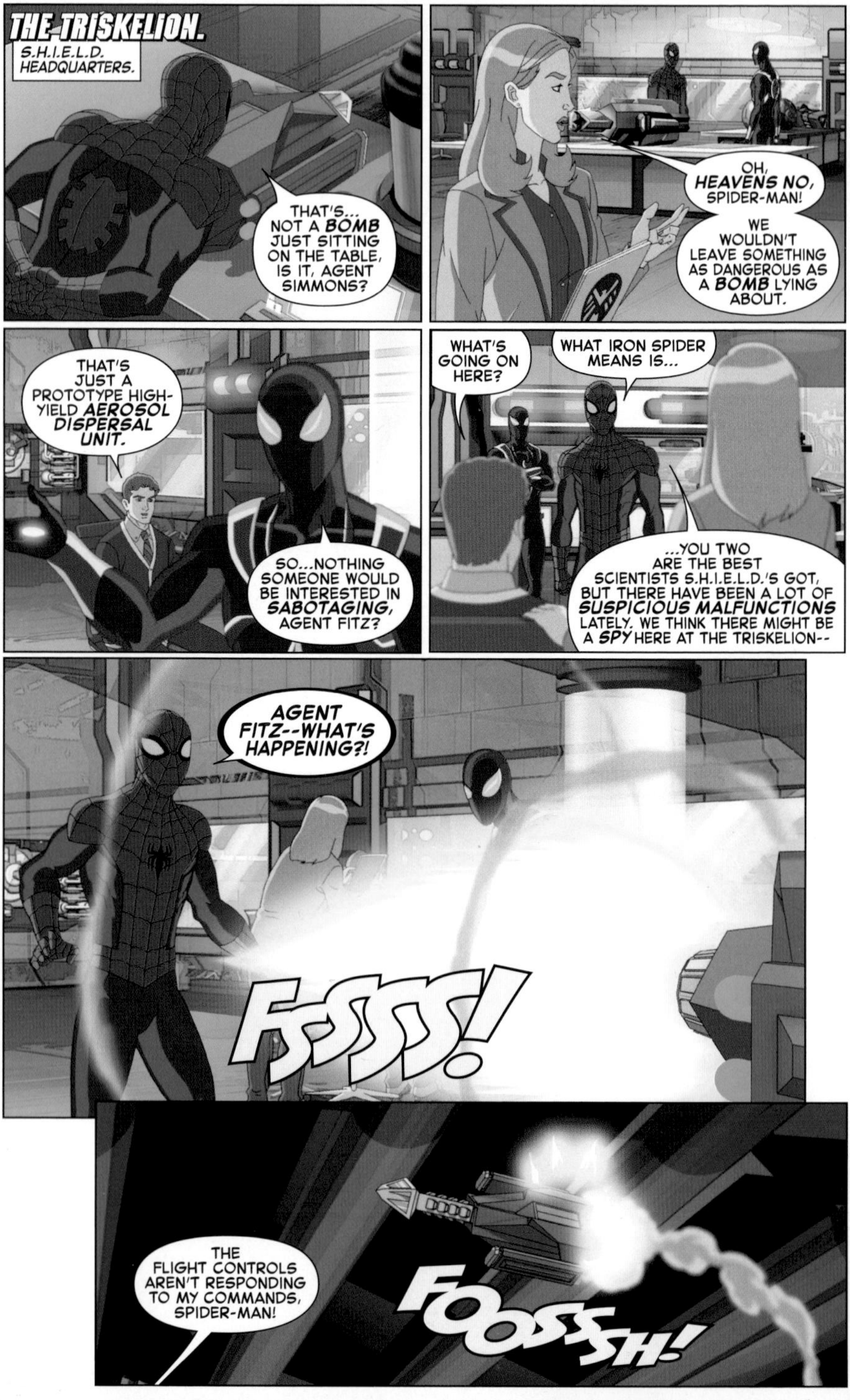
THE TRISKELION.
S.H.I.E.L.D. HEADQUARTERS.
THAT'S... NOT A BOMB JUST SITTING ON THE TABLE, IS IT, AGENT SIMMONS?
OH, HEAVENS NO, SPIDER-MAN!
WE WOULDN'T LEAVE SOMETHING AS DANGEROUS AS A BOMB LYING ABOUT.
THAT'S JUST A PROTOTYPE HIGH-YIELD AEROSOL DISPERSAL UNIT.
SO...NOTHING SOMEONE WOULD BE INTERESTED IN SABOTAGING, AGENT FITZ?
WHAT'S GOING ON HERE?
WHAT IRON SPIDER MEANS IS...
...YOU TWO ARE THE BEST SCIENTISTS S.H.I.E.L.D.'S GOT, BUT THERE HAVE BEEN A LOT OF SUSPICIOUS MALFUNCTIONS LATELY. WE THINK THERE MIGHT BE A SPY HERE AT THE TRISKELION--
AGENT FITZ--WHAT'S HAPPENING?!
FSSSS!
THE FLIGHT CONTROLS AREN'T RESPONDING TO MY COMMANDS, SPIDER-MAN!
FOOSSSH!

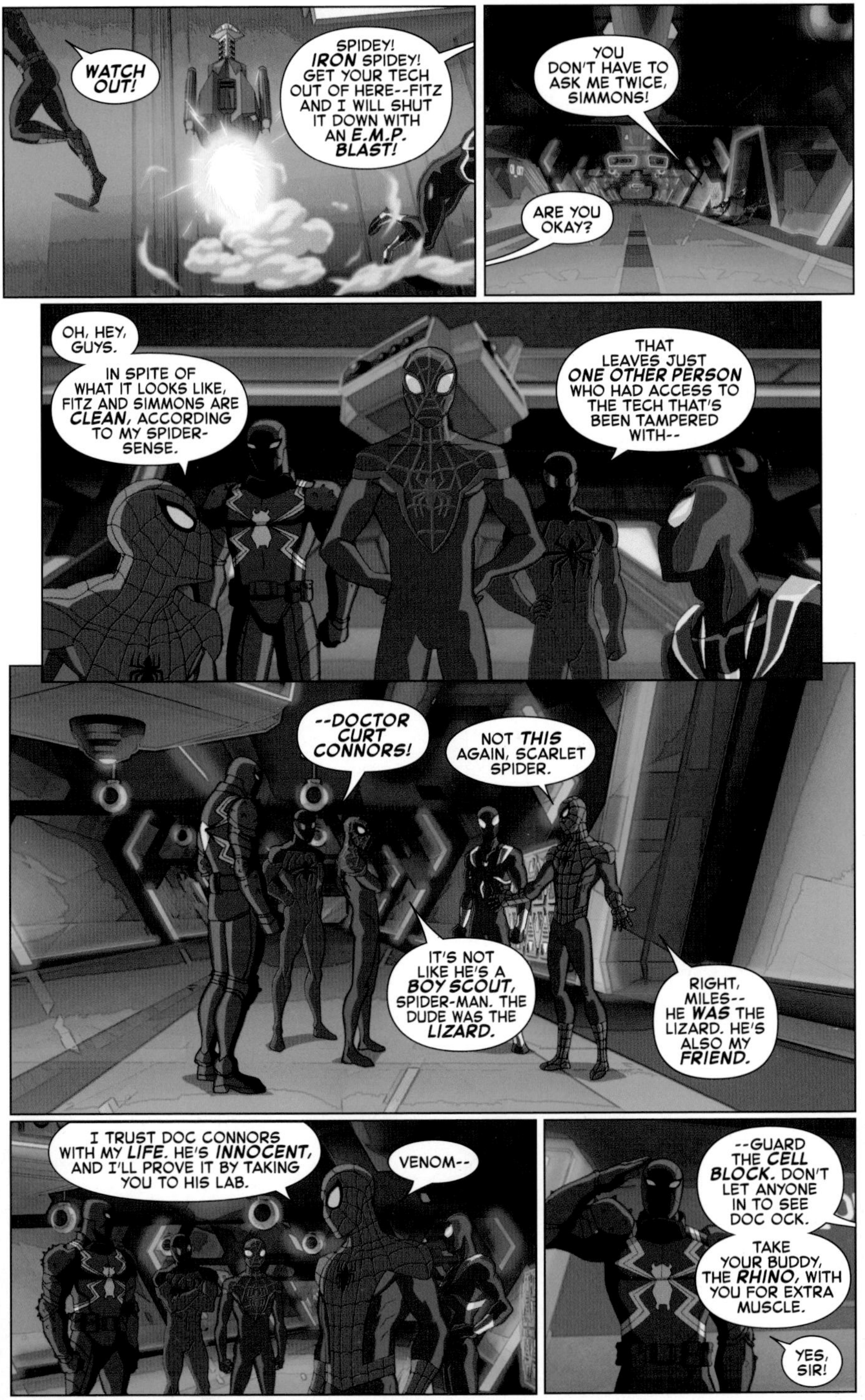
WATCH OUT!
SPIDEY! IRON SPIDEY! GET YOUR TECH OUT OF HERE--FITZ AND I WILL SHUT IT DOWN WITH AN E.M.P. BLAST!
YOU DON'T HAVE TO ASK ME TWICE, SIMMONS!
ARE YOU OKAY?
OH, HEY, GUYS.
IN SPITE OF WHAT IT LOOKS LIKE, FITZ AND SIMMONS ARE CLEAN, ACCORDING TO MY SPIDER-SENSE.
THAT LEAVES JUST ONE OTHER PERSON WHO HAD ACCESS TO THE TECH THAT'S BEEN TAMPERED WITH--
--DOCTOR CURT CONNORS!
NOT THIS AGAIN, SCARLET SPIDER.
IT'S NOT LIKE HE'S A BOY SCOUT, SPIDER-MAN. THE DUDE WAS THE LIZARD.
RIGHT, MILES-- HE WAS THE LIZARD. HE'S ALSO MY FRIEND.
I TRUST DOC CONNORS WITH MY LIFE. HE'S INNOCENT, AND I'LL PROVE IT BY TAKING YOU TO HIS LAB.
VENOM--
--GUARD THE CELL BLOCK. DON'T LET ANYONE IN TO SEE DOC OCK.
TAKE YOUR BUDDY, THE RHINO, WITH YOU FOR EXTRA MUSCLE.
YES, SIR!

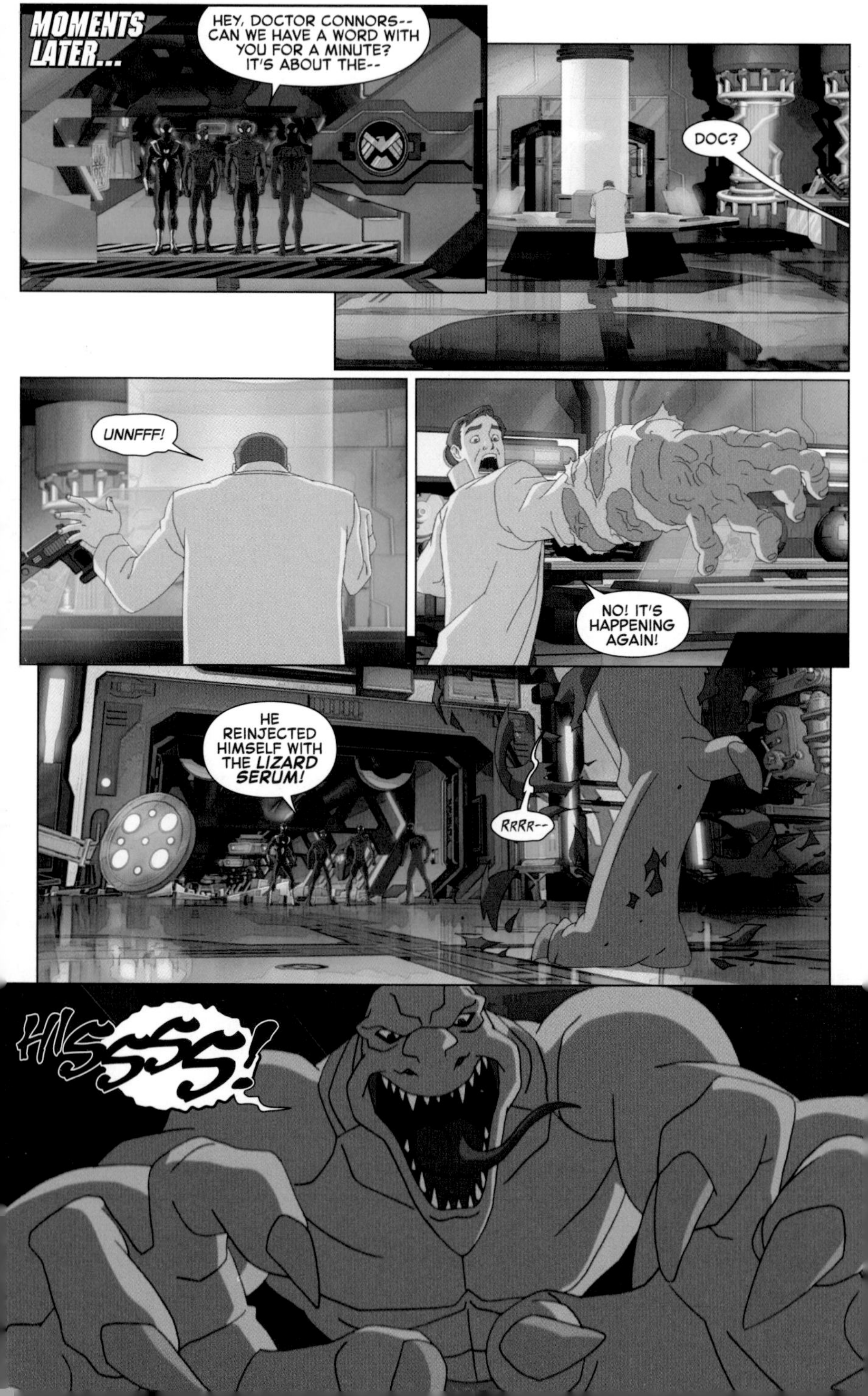
MOMENTS LATER...
HEY, DOCTOR CONNORS-- CAN WE HAVE A WORD WITH YOU FOR A MINUTE? IT'S ABOUT THE--
DOC?
UNNFFF!
NO! IT'S HAPPENING AGAIN!
HE REINJECTED HIMSELF WITH THE LIZARD SERUM!
RRRR--
HISSS!

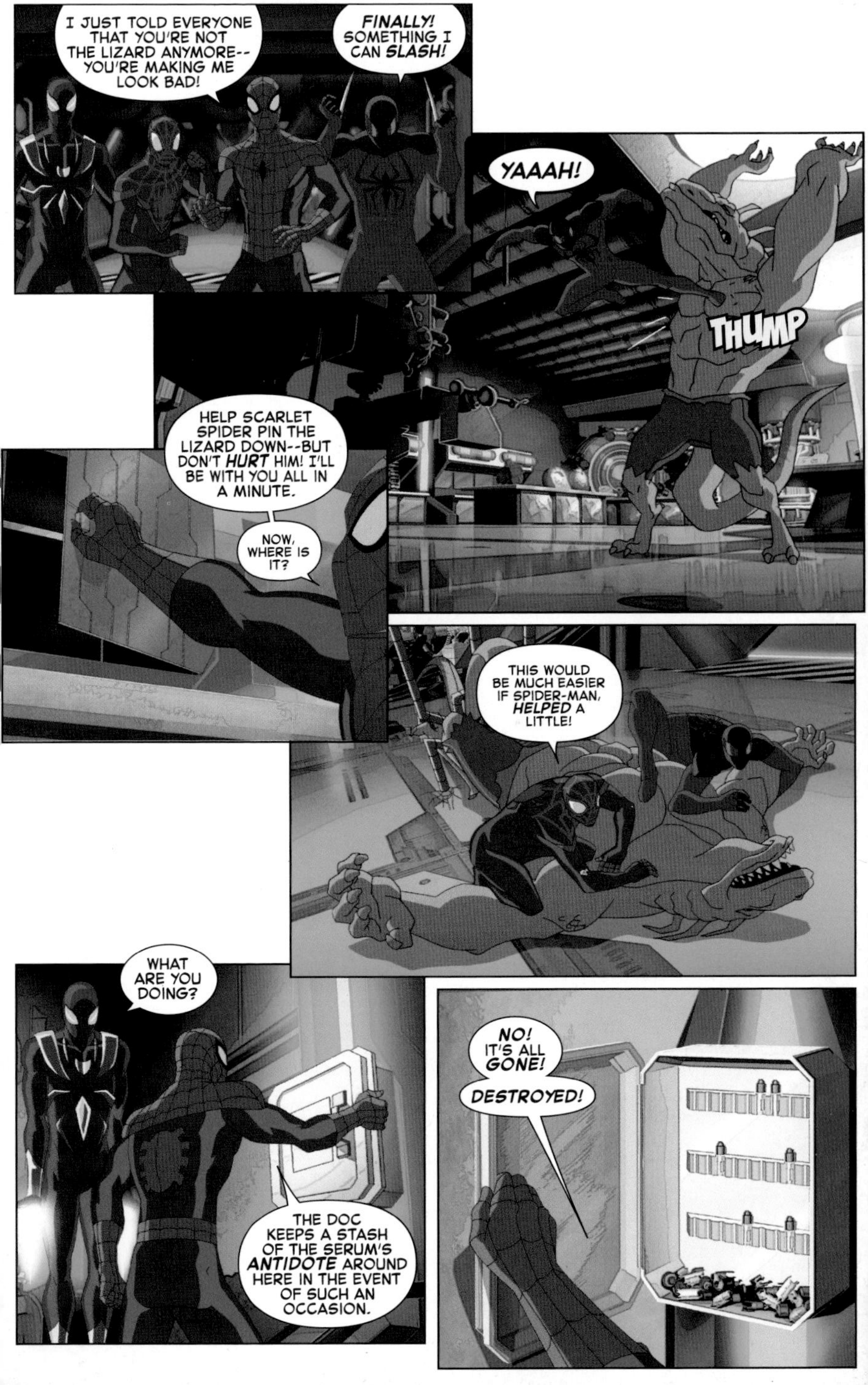
I JUST TOLD EVERYONE THAT YOU'RE NOT THE LIZARD ANYMORE--YOU'RE MAKING ME LOOK BAD!
FINALLY! SOMETHING I CAN SLASH!
YAAAH!
THUMP
HELP SCARLET SPIDER PIN THE LIZARD DOWN--BUT DON'T HURT HIM! I'LL BE WITH YOU ALL IN A MINUTE.
NOW, WHERE IS IT?
THIS WOULD BE MUCH EASIER IF SPIDER-MAN, HELPED A LITTLE!
WHAT ARE YOU DOING?
THE DOC KEEPS A STASH OF THE SERUM'S ANTIDOTE AROUND HERE IN THE EVENT OF SUCH AN OCCASION.
NO! IT'S ALL GONE!
DESTROYED!

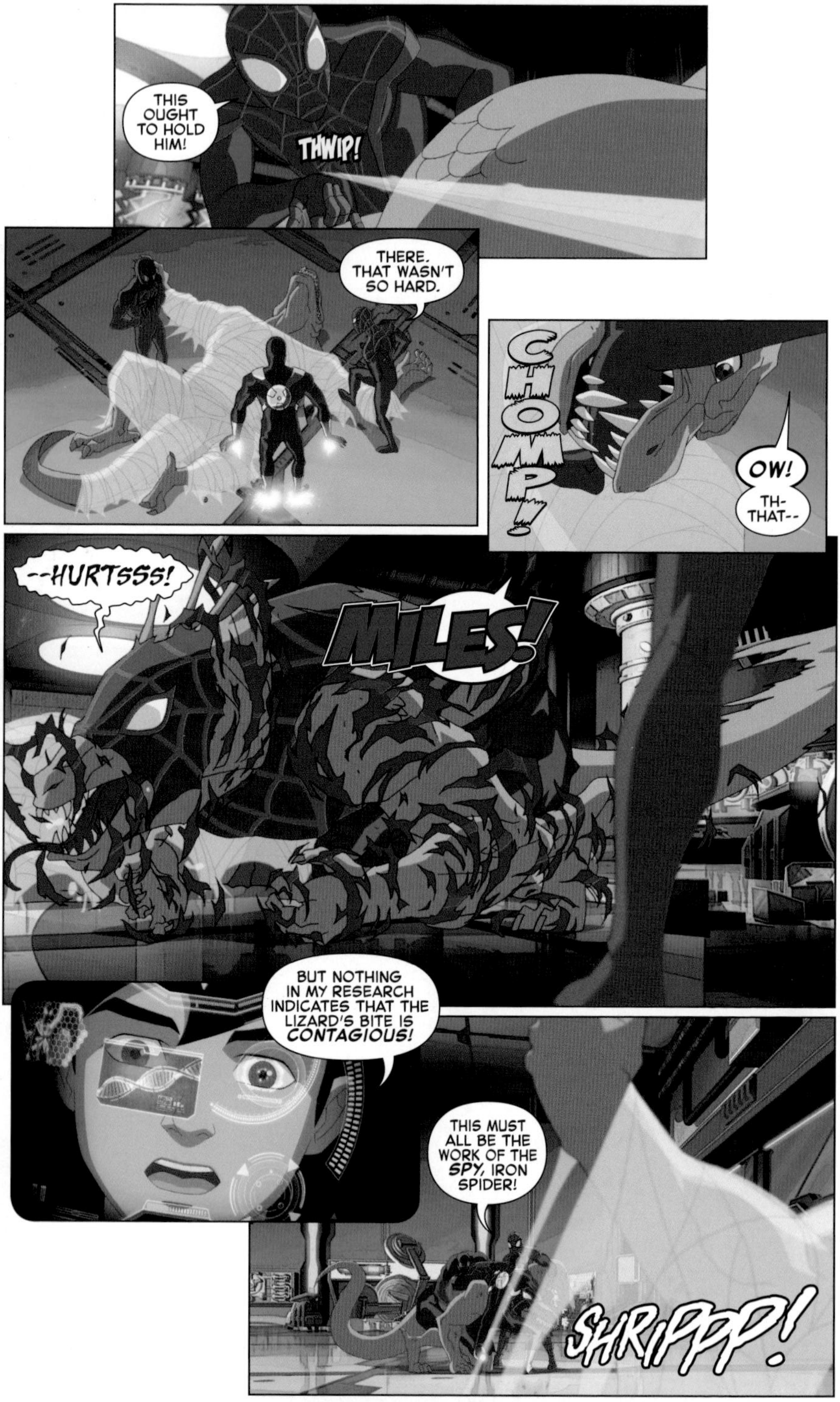

THIS OUGHT TO HOLD HIM!
THWIP!
THERE. THAT WASN'T SO HARD.
CHOMP!
OW!
TH- THAT--
--HURTSSS!
MILES!
BUT NOTHING IN MY RESEARCH INDICATES THAT THE LIZARD'S BITE IS CONTAGIOUS!
THIS MUST ALL BE THE WORK OF THE SPY, IRON SPIDER!
SHRIPPP!

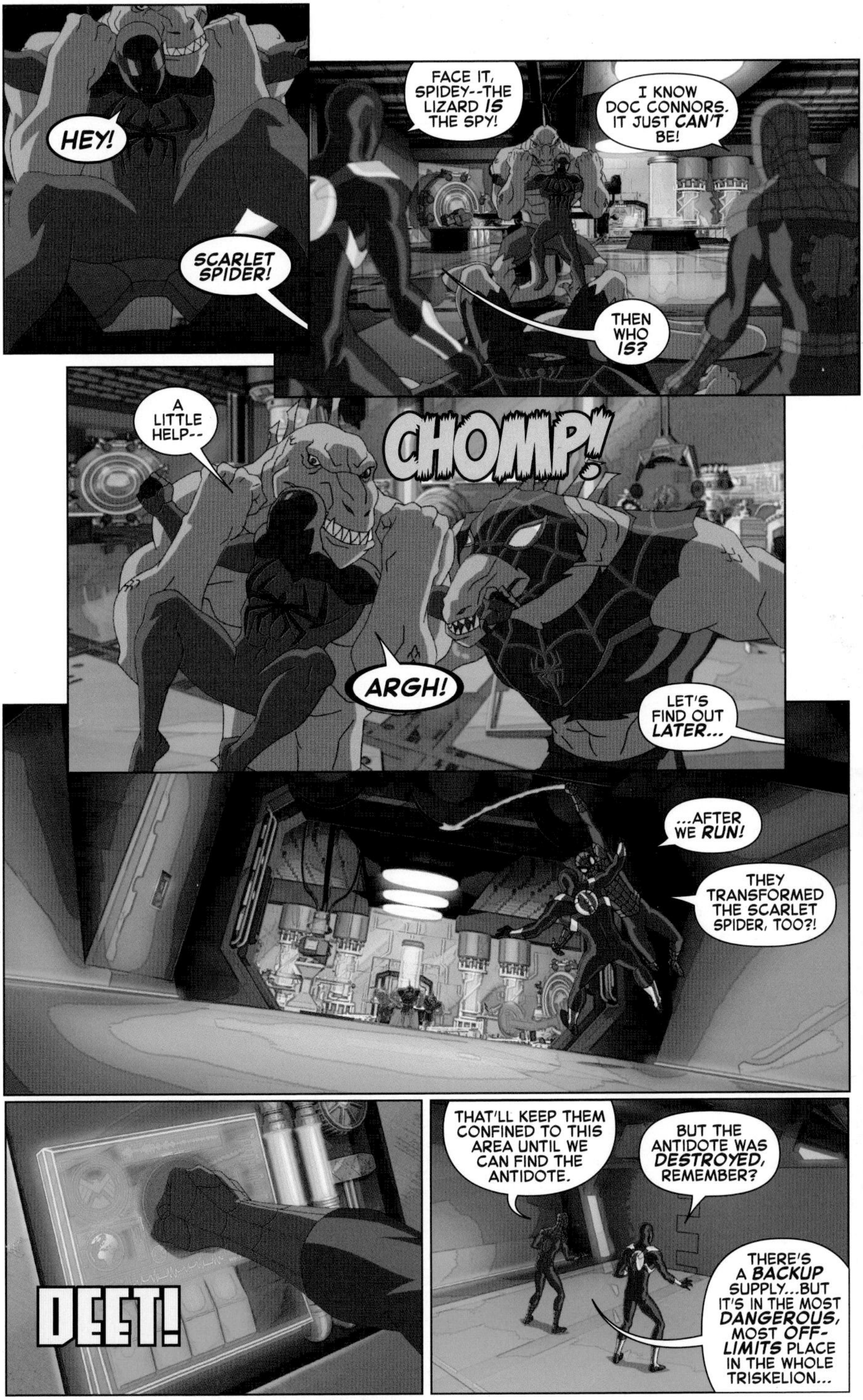
HEY!
SCARLET SPIDER!
FACE IT, SPIDEY--THE LIZARD IS THE SPY!
I KNOW DOC CONNORS. IT JUST CAN'T BE!
THEN WHO IS?
A LITTLE HELP--
CHOMP!
ARGH!
LET'S FIND OUT LATER...
...AFTER WE RUN!
THEY TRANSFORMED THE SCARLET SPIDER, TOO?!
DEET!
THAT'LL KEEP THEM CONFINED TO THIS AREA UNTIL WE CAN FIND THE ANTIDOTE.
BUT THE ANTIDOTE WAS DESTROYED, REMEMBER?
THERE'S A BACKUP SUPPLY...BUT IT'S IN THE MOST DANGEROUS, MOST OFF-LIMITS PLACE IN THE WHOLE TRISKELION...

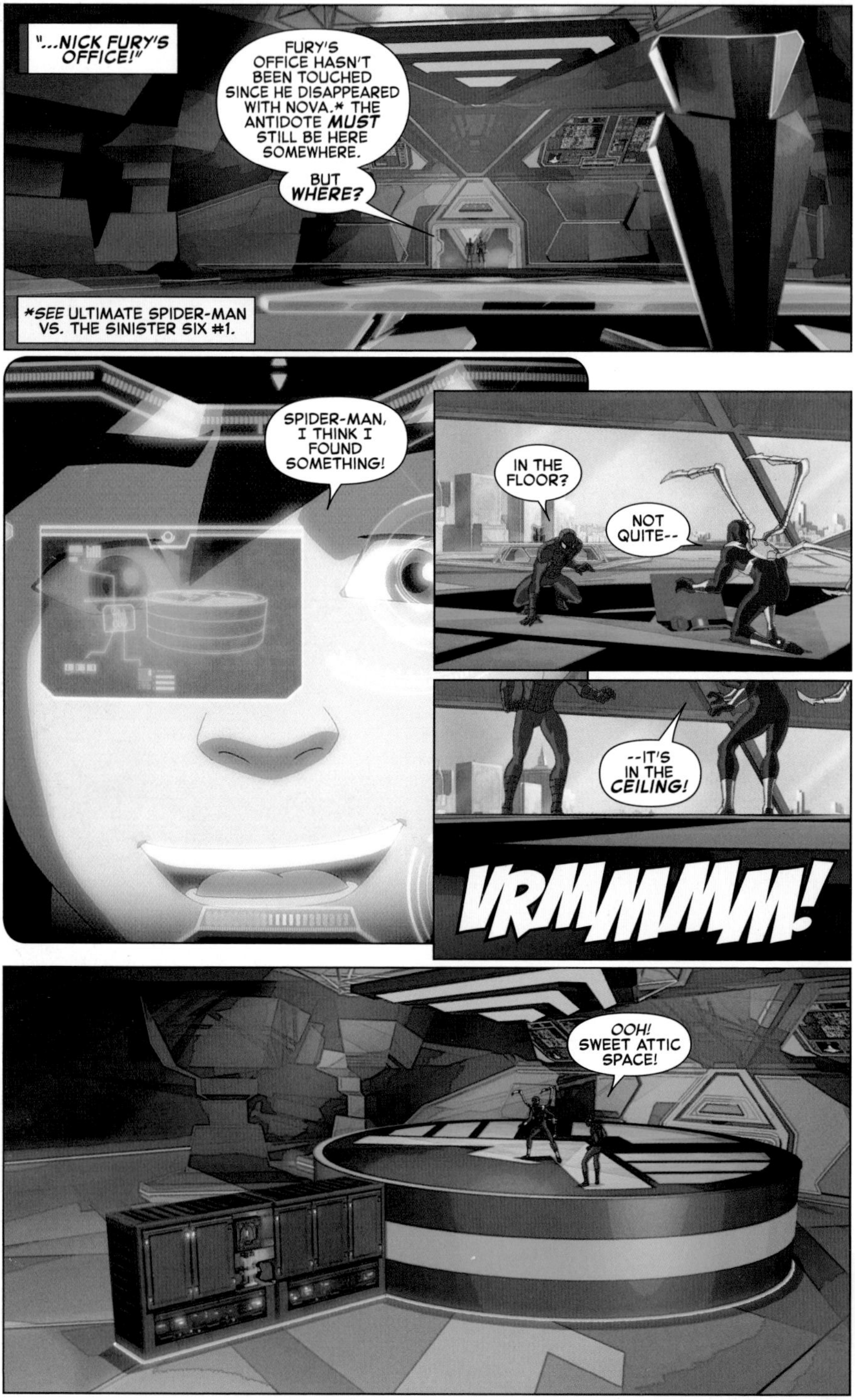
"...NICK FURY'S OFFICE!"
FURY'S OFFICE HASN'T BEEN TOUCHED SINCE HE DISAPPEARED WITH NOVA.* THE ANTIDOTE MUST STILL BE HERE SOMEWHERE.
BUT WHERE?
*SEE ULTIMATE SPIDER-MAN VS. THE SINISTER SIX #1.
SPIDER-MAN, I THINK I FOUND SOMETHING!
IN THE FLOOR?
NOT QUITE--
--IT'S IN THE CEILING!
VRMMMM!
OOH! SWEET ATTIC SPACE!

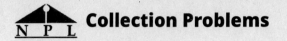 **Collection Problems**

HOLDS ON THIS ITEM ☐

CuS STAFF _____UA_____ DATE _1/16_ BDG _NL_

　　STATUS SET TO WORKROOM: ☑

AS/CH STAFF_____ DATE_____ BDG_____

　　STATUS SET TO MENDING: ☐

MENDING
ITEM BARCODE: _4415   8276_

EXPLAIN:

　　　loose pages

DONATION
NEW ☐　ADD BIB:_____ BDG:_____

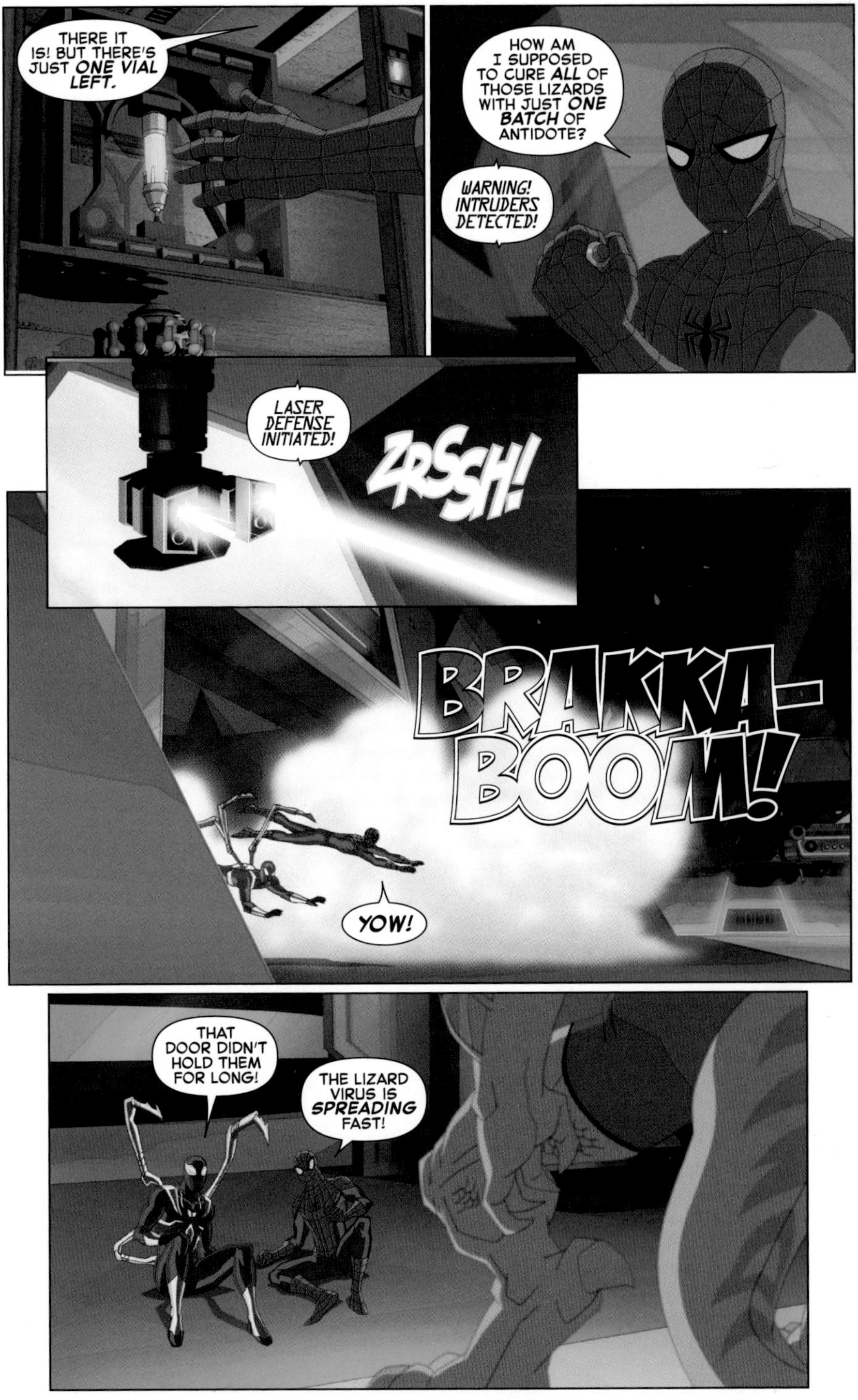
THERE IT IS! BUT THERE'S JUST ONE VIAL LEFT.
HOW AM I SUPPOSED TO CURE ALL OF THOSE LIZARDS WITH JUST ONE BATCH OF ANTIDOTE?
WARNING! INTRUDERS DETECTED!
LASER DEFENSE INITIATED!
ZRSSH!
BRAKKA-BOOM!
YOW!
THAT DOOR DIDN'T HOLD THEM FOR LONG!
THE LIZARD VIRUS IS SPREADING FAST!

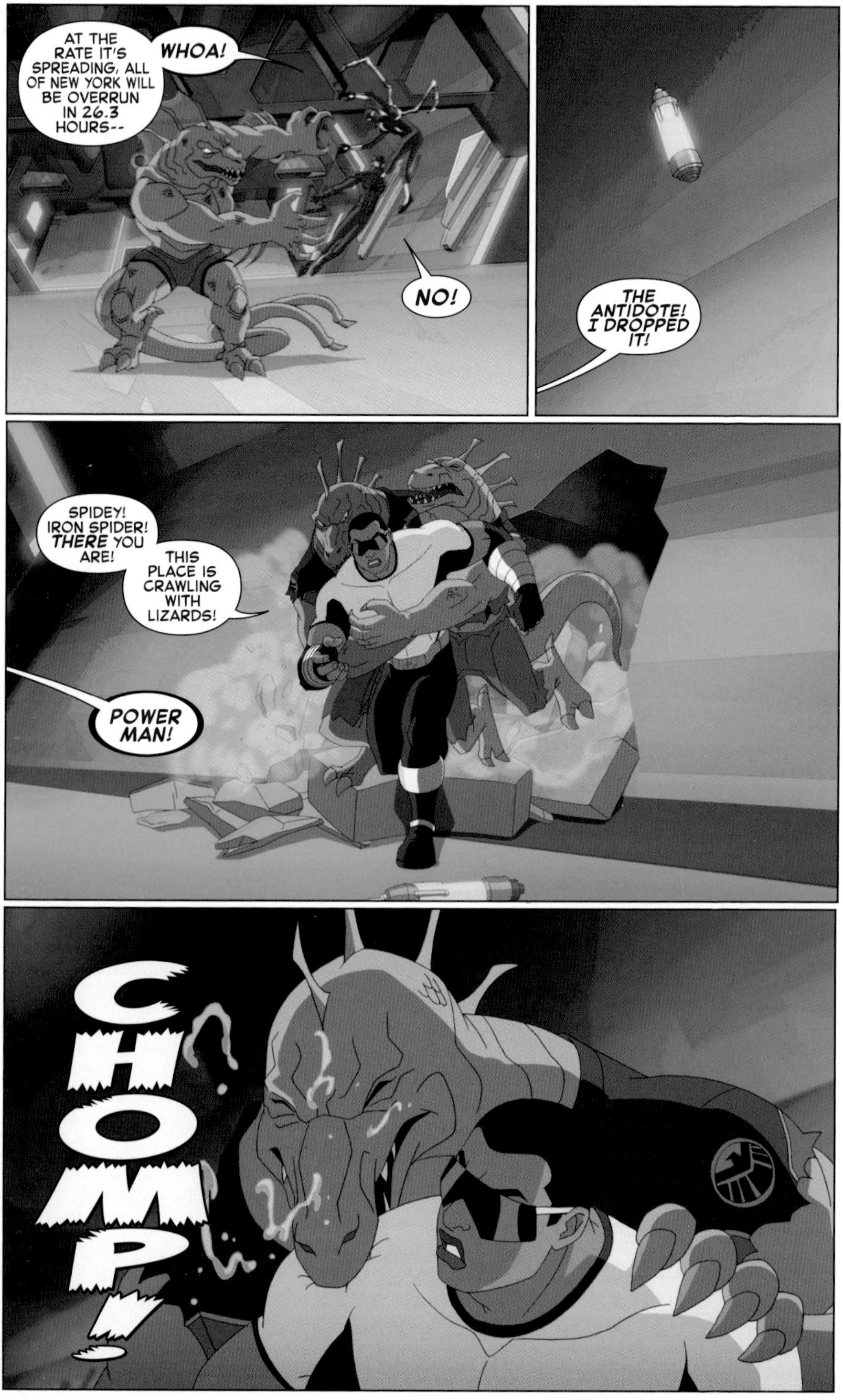
AT THE RATE IT'S SPREADING, ALL OF NEW YORK WILL BE OVERRUN IN 26.3 HOURS--
WHOA!
NO!
THE ANTIDOTE! I DROPPED IT!
SPIDEY! IRON SPIDER! THERE YOU ARE!
THIS PLACE IS CRAWLING WITH LIZARDS!
POWER MAN!
CHOMP!

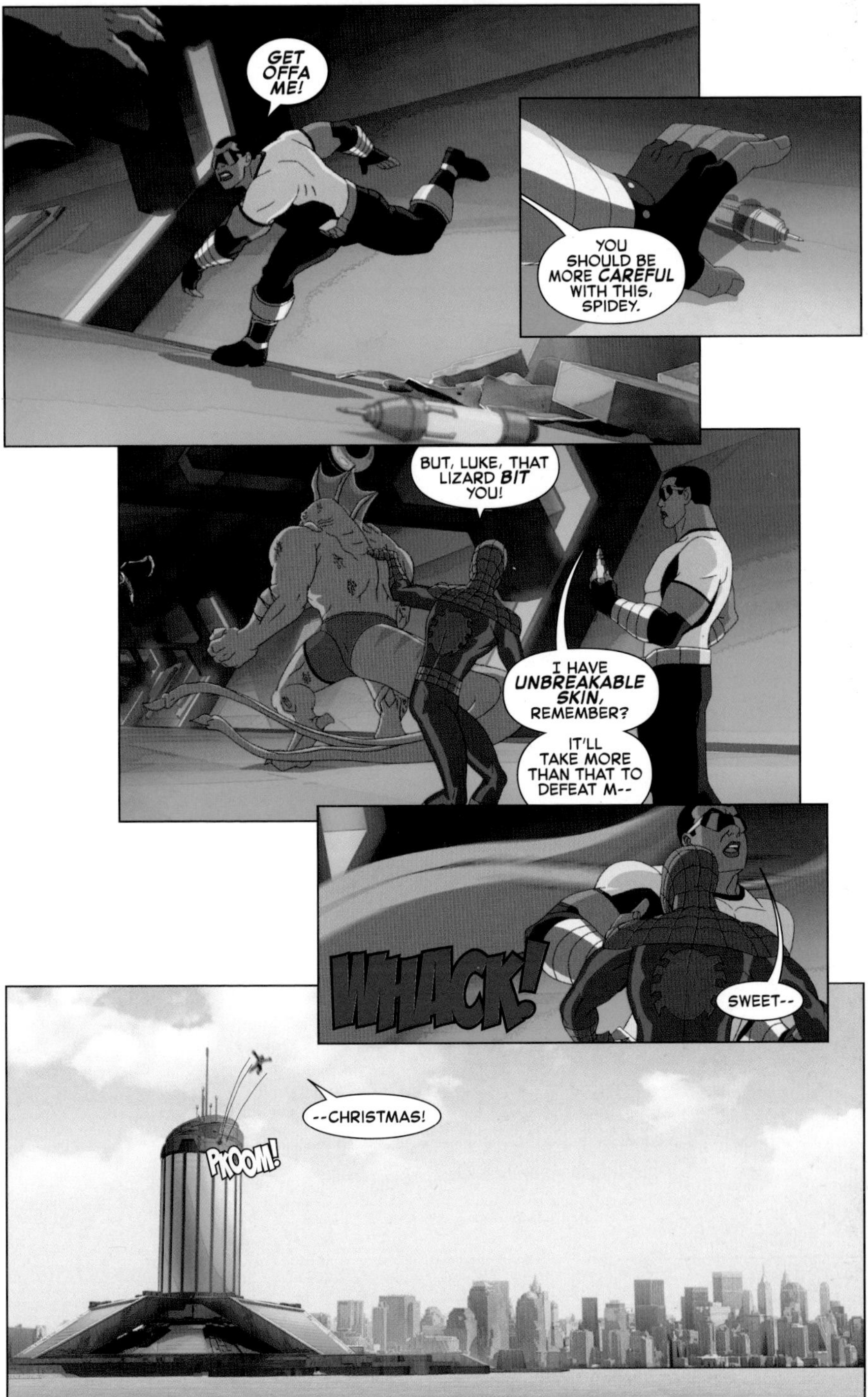
GET OFFA ME!
YOU SHOULD BE MORE CAREFUL WITH THIS, SPIDEY.
BUT, LUKE, THAT LIZARD BIT YOU!
I HAVE UNBREAKABLE SKIN, REMEMBER?
IT'LL TAKE MORE THAN THAT TO DEFEAT M--
WHACK!
SWEET--
--CHRISTMAS!
PKOOM!

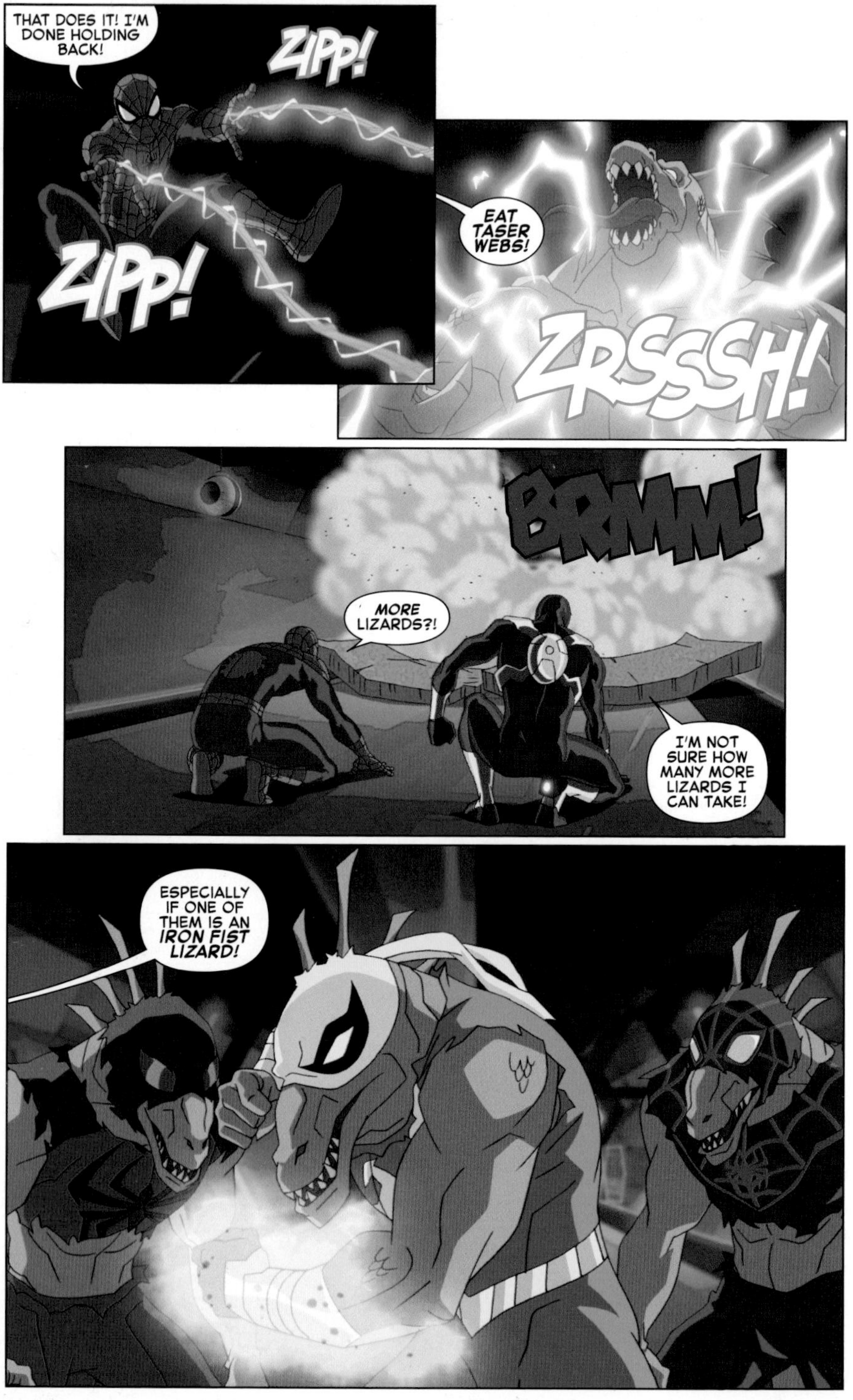
THAT DOES IT! I'M DONE HOLDING BACK!
ZIPP!
ZIPP!
EAT TASER WEBS!
ZRSSSH!
BRMMM!
MORE LIZARDS?!
I'M NOT SURE HOW MANY MORE LIZARDS I CAN TAKE!
ESPECIALLY IF ONE OF THEM IS AN IRON FIST LIZARD!

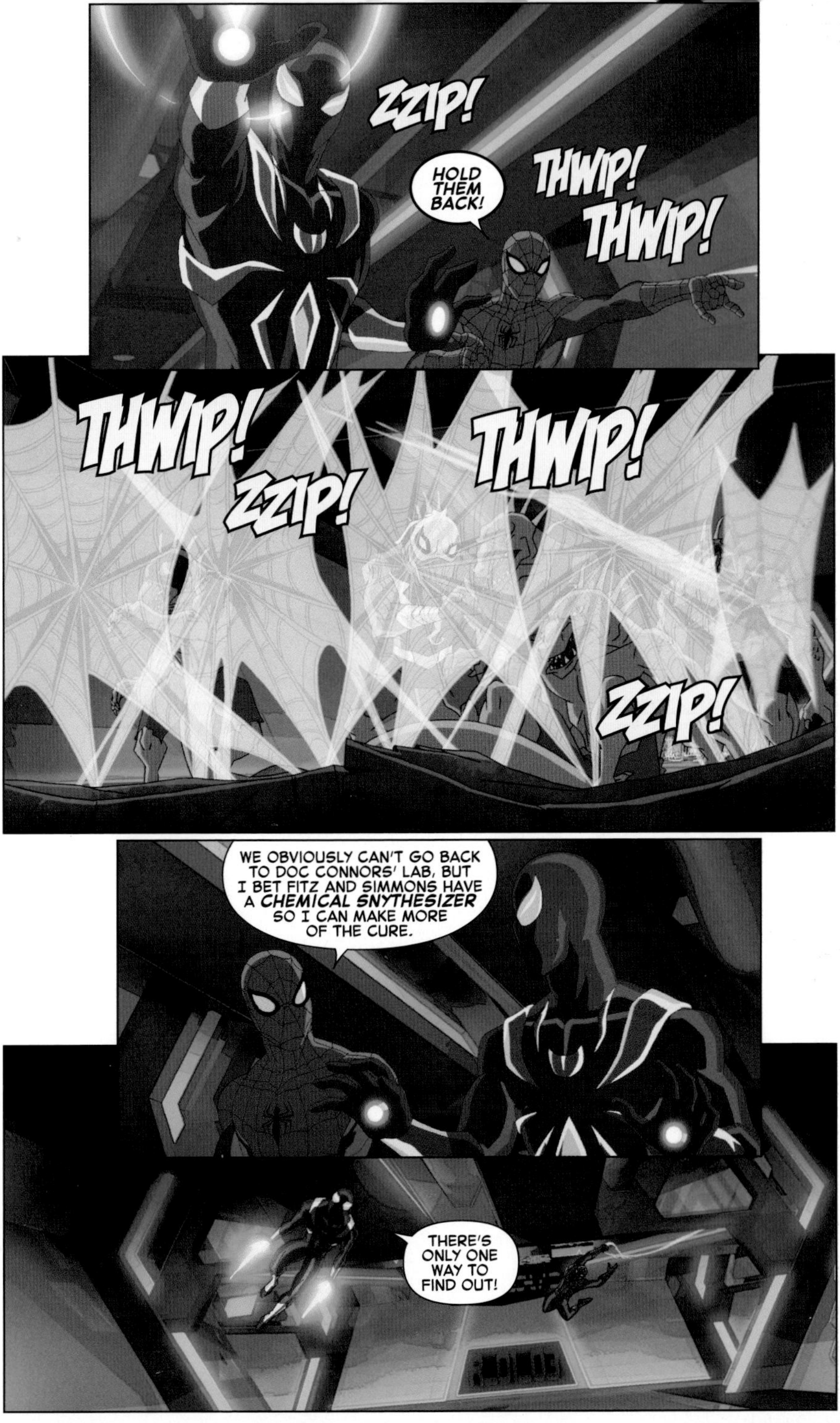
ZZIP!
HOLD THEM BACK!
THWIP!
THWIP!
THWIP!
ZZIP!
THWIP!
ZZIP!
WE OBVIOUSLY CAN'T GO BACK TO DOC CONNORS' LAB, BUT I BET FITZ AND SIMMONS HAVE A *CHEMICAL SNYTHESIZER* SO I CAN MAKE MORE OF THE CURE.
THERE'S ONLY ONE WAY TO FIND OUT!

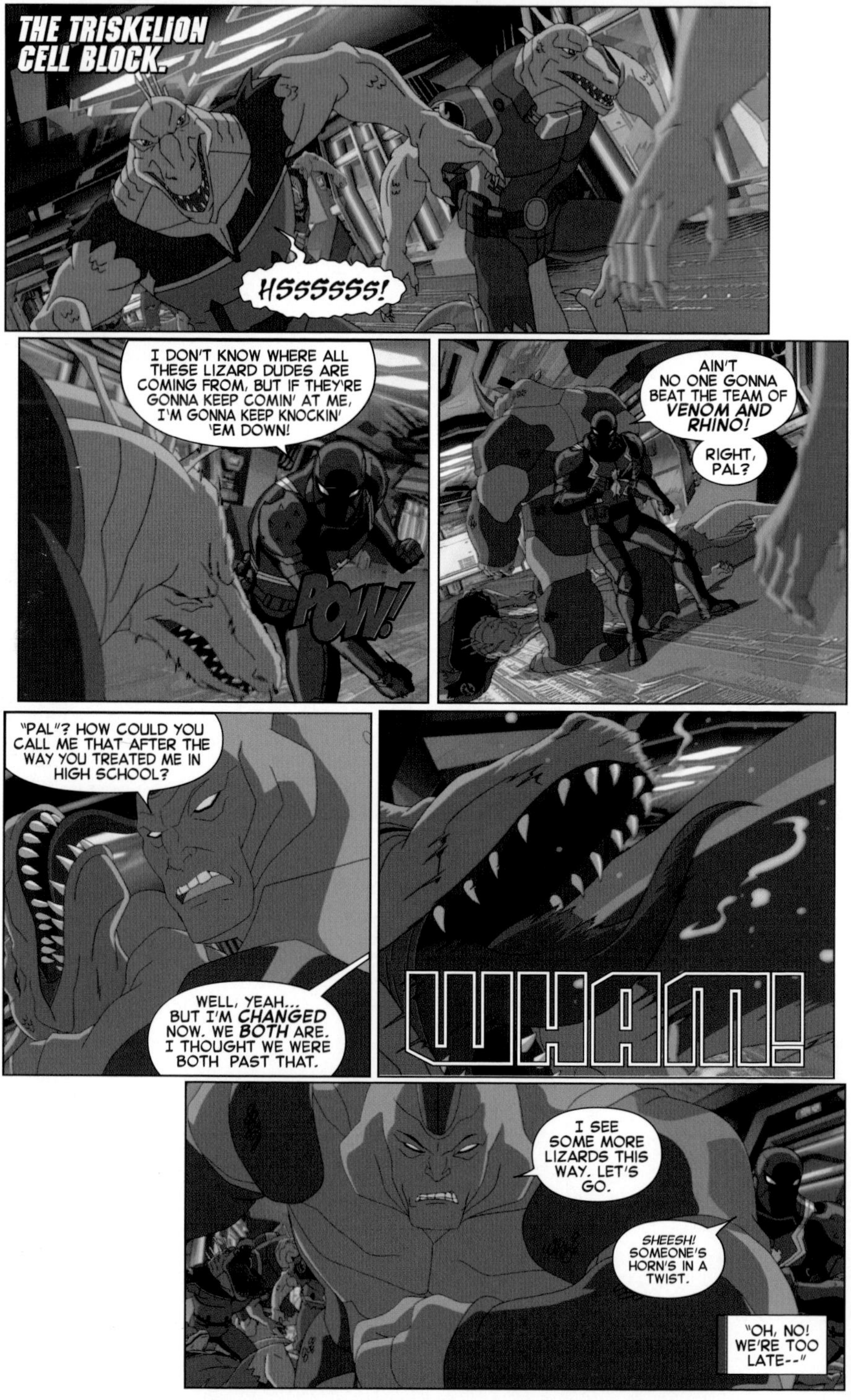
THE TRISKELION CELL BLOCK.
HSSSSSS!
I DON'T KNOW WHERE ALL THESE LIZARD DUDES ARE COMING FROM, BUT IF THEY'RE GONNA KEEP COMIN' AT ME, I'M GONNA KEEP KNOCKIN' 'EM DOWN!
POW!
AIN'T NO ONE GONNA BEAT THE TEAM OF VENOM AND RHINO!
RIGHT, PAL?
"PAL"? HOW COULD YOU CALL ME THAT AFTER THE WAY YOU TREATED ME IN HIGH SCHOOL?
WELL, YEAH... BUT I'M CHANGED NOW. WE BOTH ARE. I THOUGHT WE WERE BOTH PAST THAT.
WHAM!
I SEE SOME MORE LIZARDS THIS WAY. LET'S GO.
SHEESH! SOMEONE'S HORN'S IN A TWIST.
"OH, NO! WE'RE TOO LATE--"

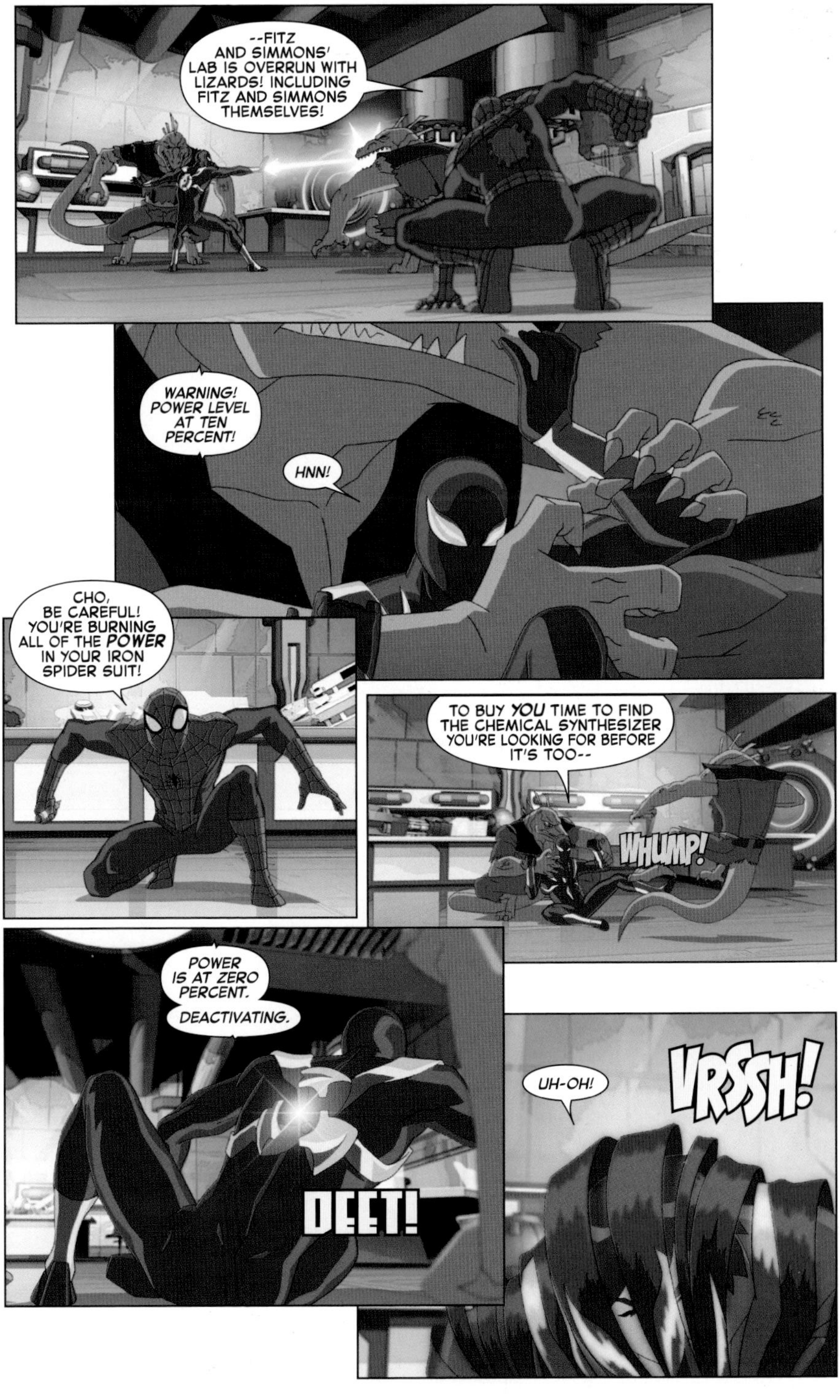
--FITZ AND SIMMONS' LAB IS OVERRUN WITH LIZARDS! INCLUDING FITZ AND SIMMONS THEMSELVES!
WARNING! POWER LEVEL AT TEN PERCENT!
HNN!
CHO, BE CAREFUL! YOU'RE BURNING ALL OF THE POWER IN YOUR IRON SPIDER SUIT!
TO BUY YOU TIME TO FIND THE CHEMICAL SYNTHESIZER YOU'RE LOOKING FOR BEFORE IT'S TOO--
WHUMP!
POWER IS AT ZERO PERCENT.
DEACTIVATING.
DEET!
UH-OH!
VRSSH!

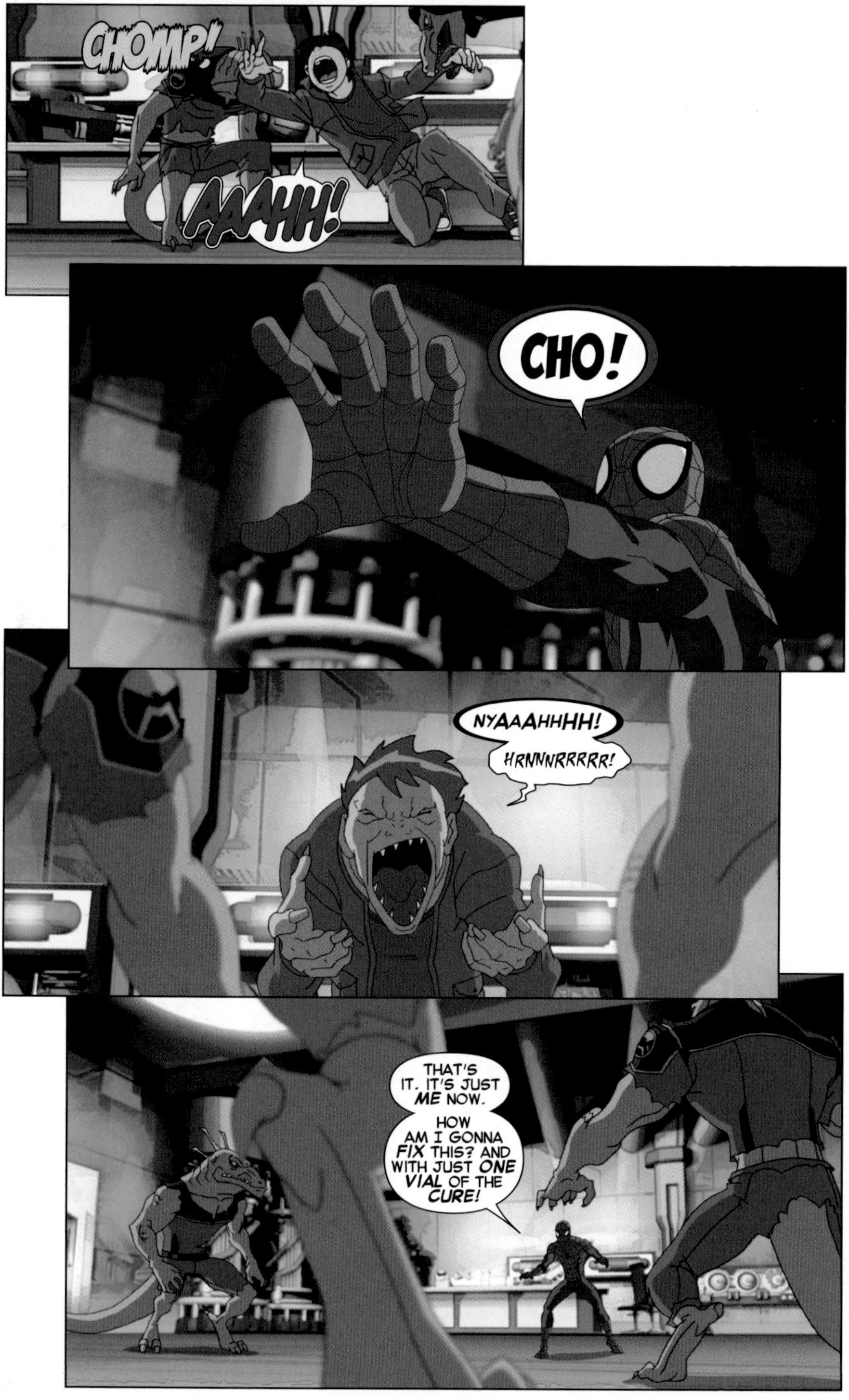
CHOMP!
AAAHH!
CHO!
NYAAAHHHH!
HRNNNRRRRR!
THAT'S IT. IT'S JUST ME NOW.
HOW AM I GONNA FIX THIS? AND WITH JUST ONE VIAL OF THE CURE!

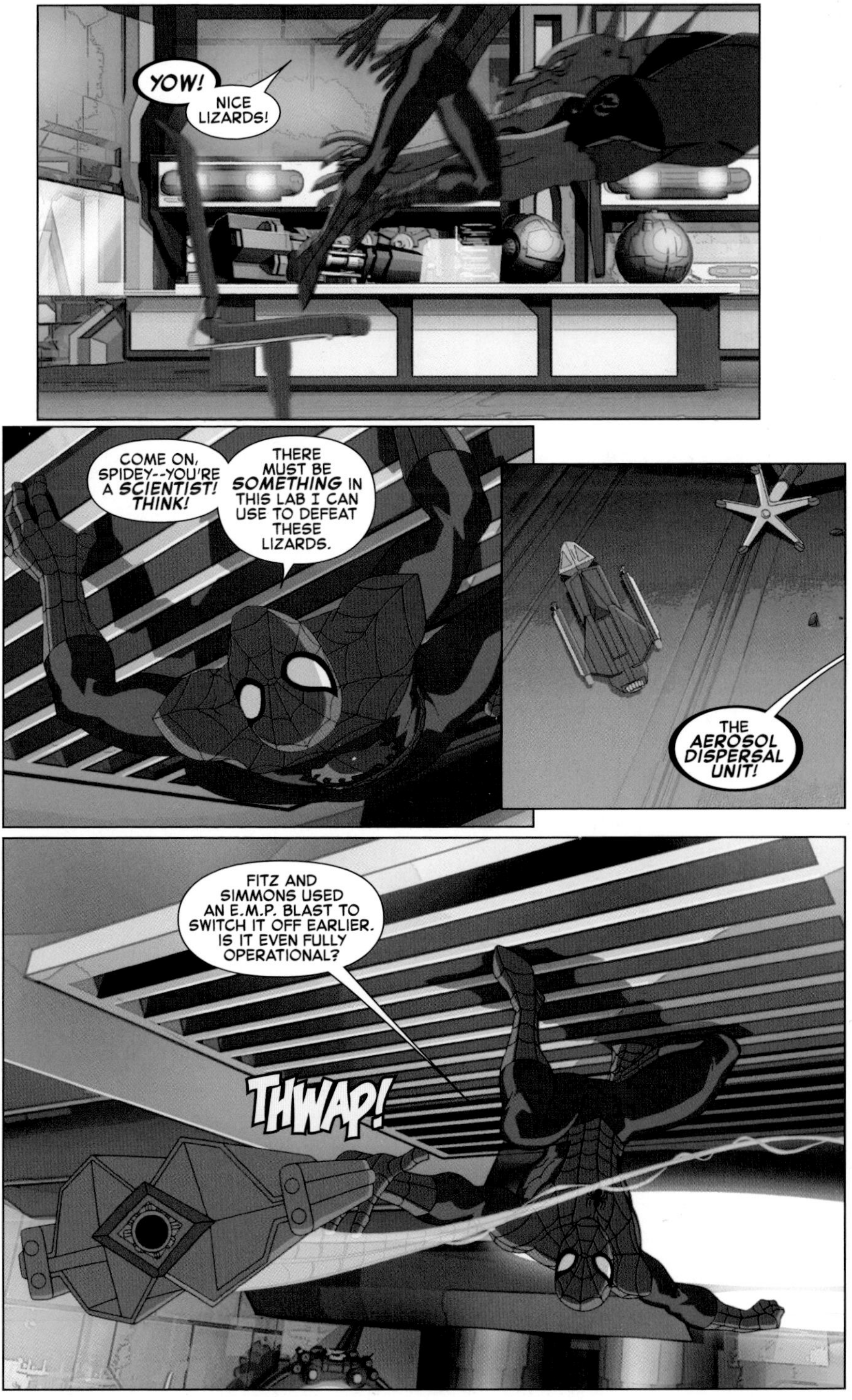
YOW!
NICE LIZARDS!
COME ON, SPIDEY--YOU'RE A SCIENTIST! THINK!
THERE MUST BE SOMETHING IN THIS LAB I CAN USE TO DEFEAT THESE LIZARDS.
THE AEROSOL DISPERSAL UNIT!
FITZ AND SIMMONS USED AN E.M.P. BLAST TO SWITCH IT OFF EARLIER. IS IT EVEN FULLY OPERATIONAL?
THWAP!

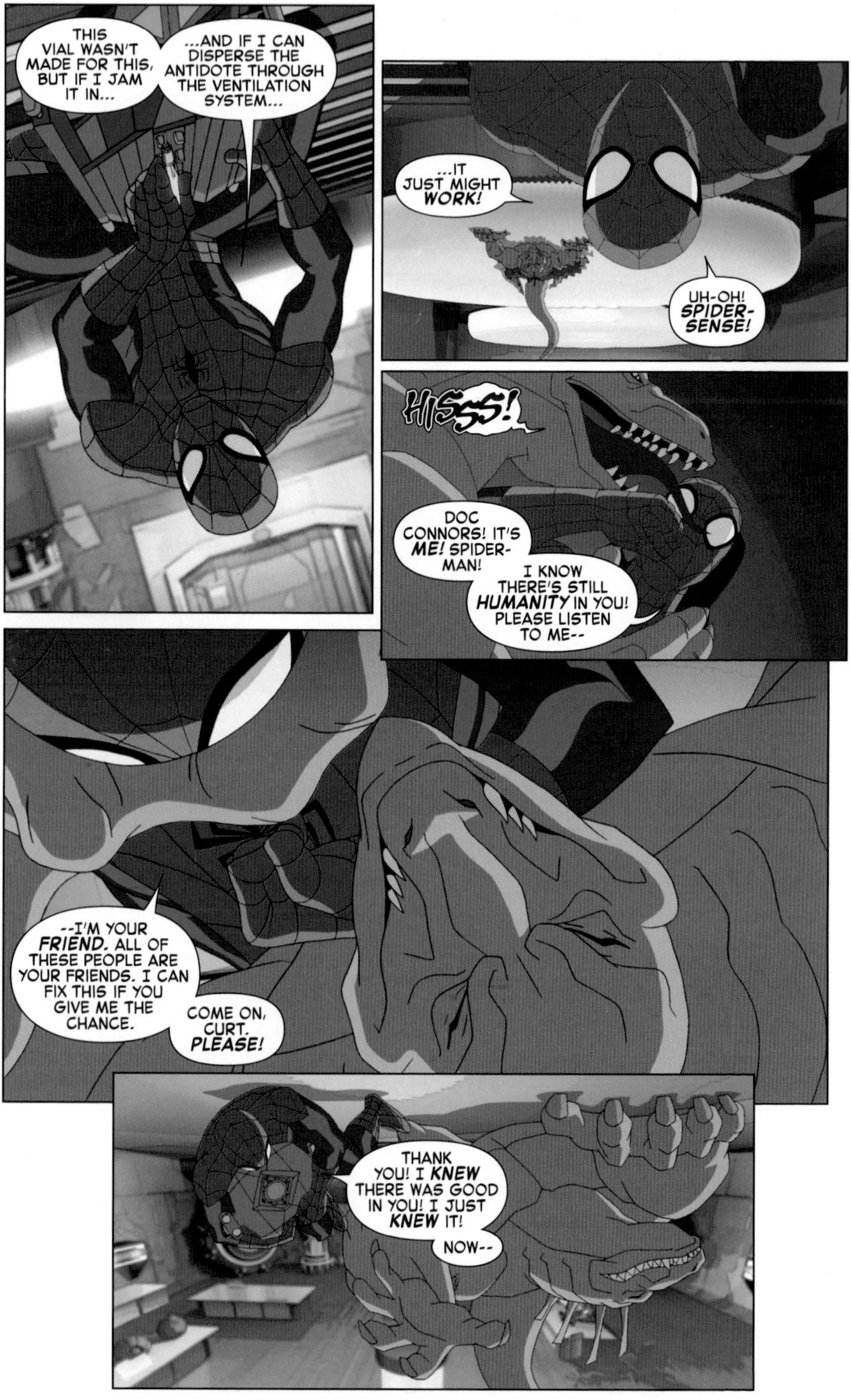
THIS VIAL WASN'T MADE FOR THIS, BUT IF I JAM IT IN...
...AND IF I CAN DISPERSE THE ANTIDOTE THROUGH THE VENTILATION SYSTEM...
...IT JUST MIGHT WORK!
UH-OH! SPIDER-SENSE!
HISSS!
DOC CONNORS! IT'S ME! SPIDER-MAN!
I KNOW THERE'S STILL HUMANITY IN YOU! PLEASE LISTEN TO ME--
--I'M YOUR FRIEND. ALL OF THESE PEOPLE ARE YOUR FRIENDS. I CAN FIX THIS IF YOU GIVE ME THE CHANCE.
COME ON, CURT. PLEASE!
THANK YOU! I KNEW THERE WAS GOOD IN YOU! I JUST KNEW IT!
NOW--

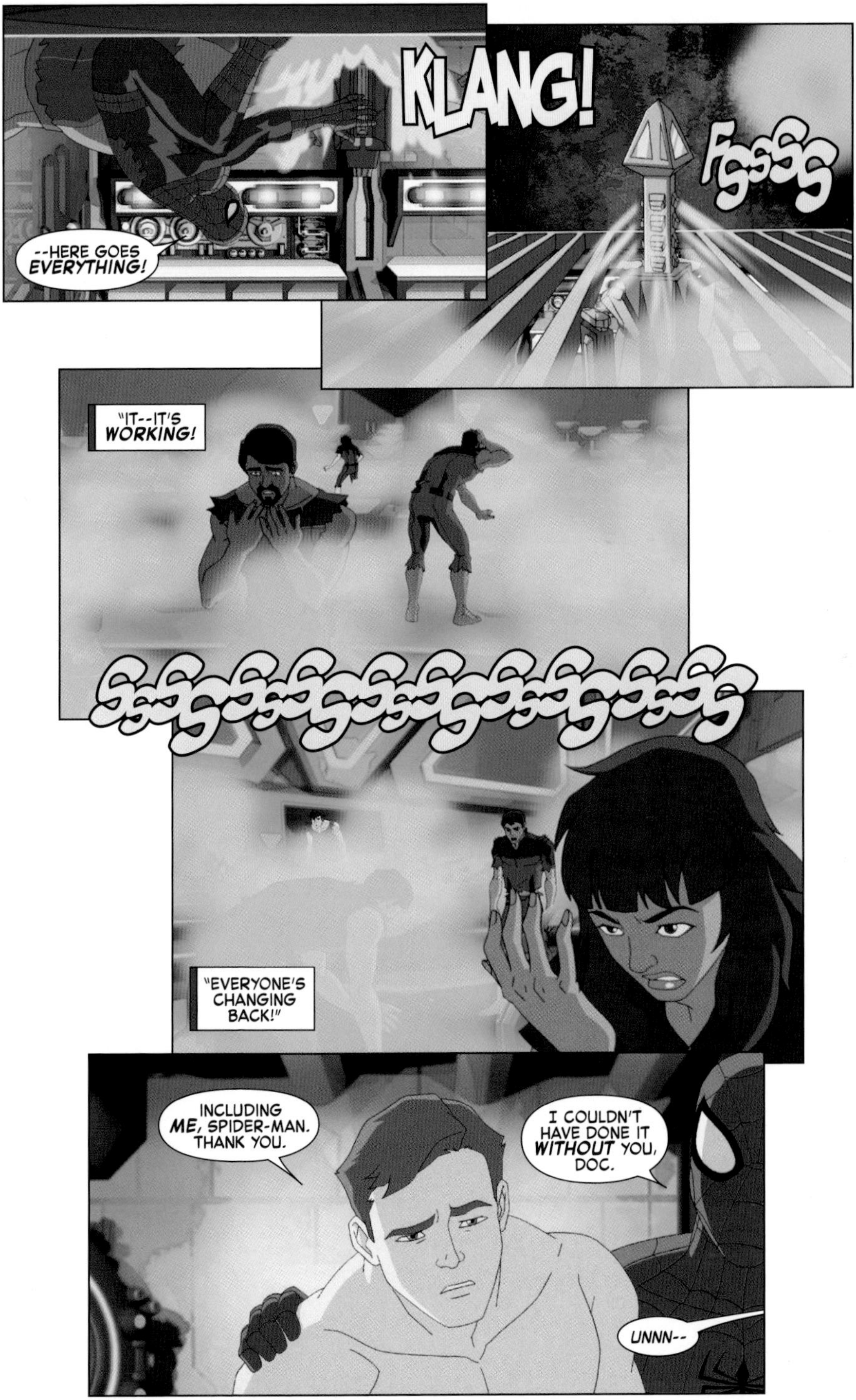
--HERE GOES EVERYTHING!
KLANG!
FSSSS
"IT--IT'S WORKING!
SSSSSSSSSSSSSSSSSSS
"EVERYONE'S CHANGING BACK!"
INCLUDING ME, SPIDER-MAN. THANK YOU.
I COULDN'T HAVE DONE IT WITHOUT YOU, DOC.
UNNN--

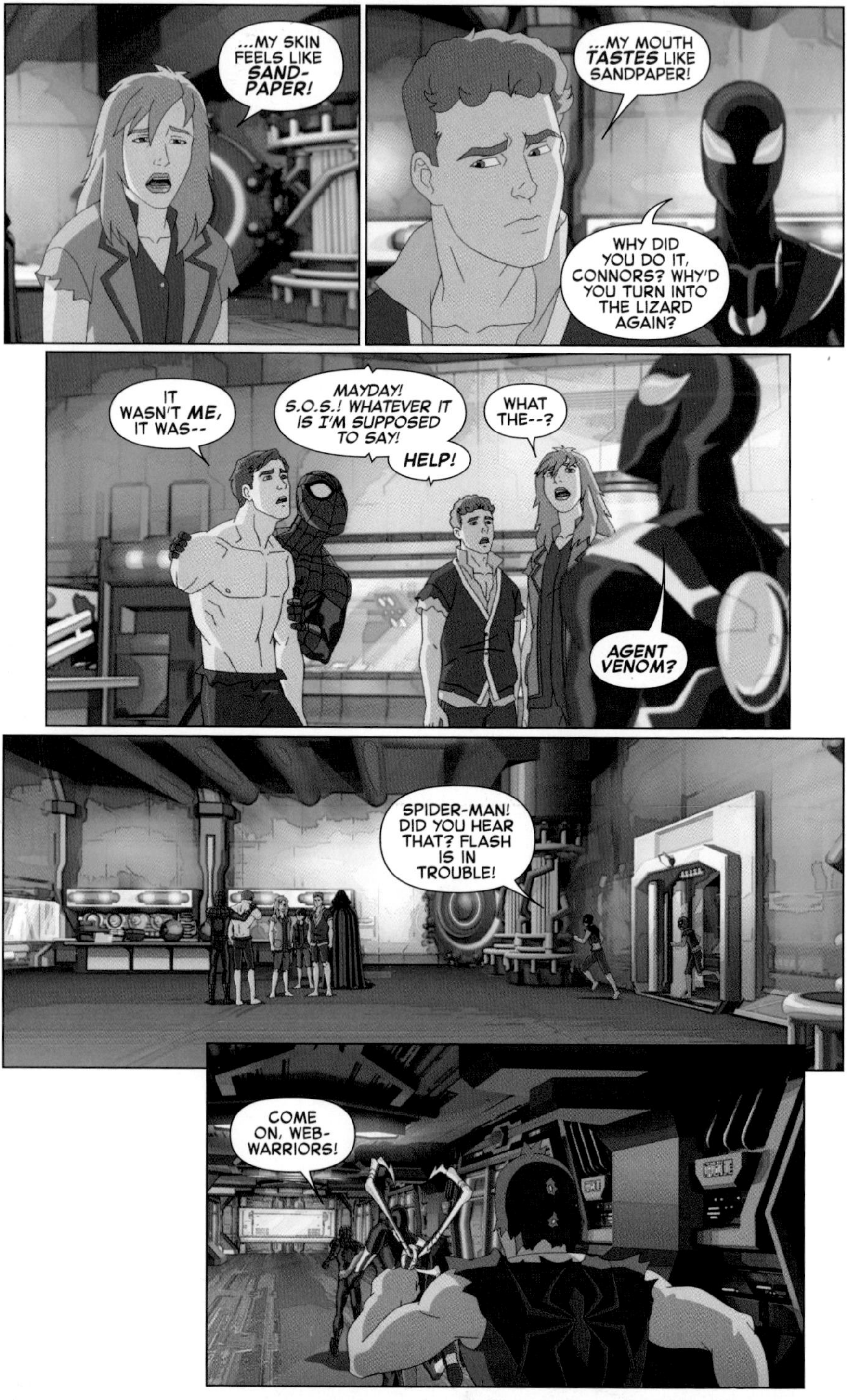
...MY SKIN FEELS LIKE SANDPAPER!
...MY MOUTH TASTES LIKE SANDPAPER!
WHY DID YOU DO IT, CONNORS? WHY'D YOU TURN INTO THE LIZARD AGAIN?
IT WASN'T ME, IT WAS--
MAYDAY! S.O.S.! WHATEVER IT IS I'M SUPPOSED TO SAY! HELP!
WHAT THE--?
AGENT VENOM?
SPIDER-MAN! DID YOU HEAR THAT? FLASH IS IN TROUBLE!
COME ON, WEB-WARRIORS!

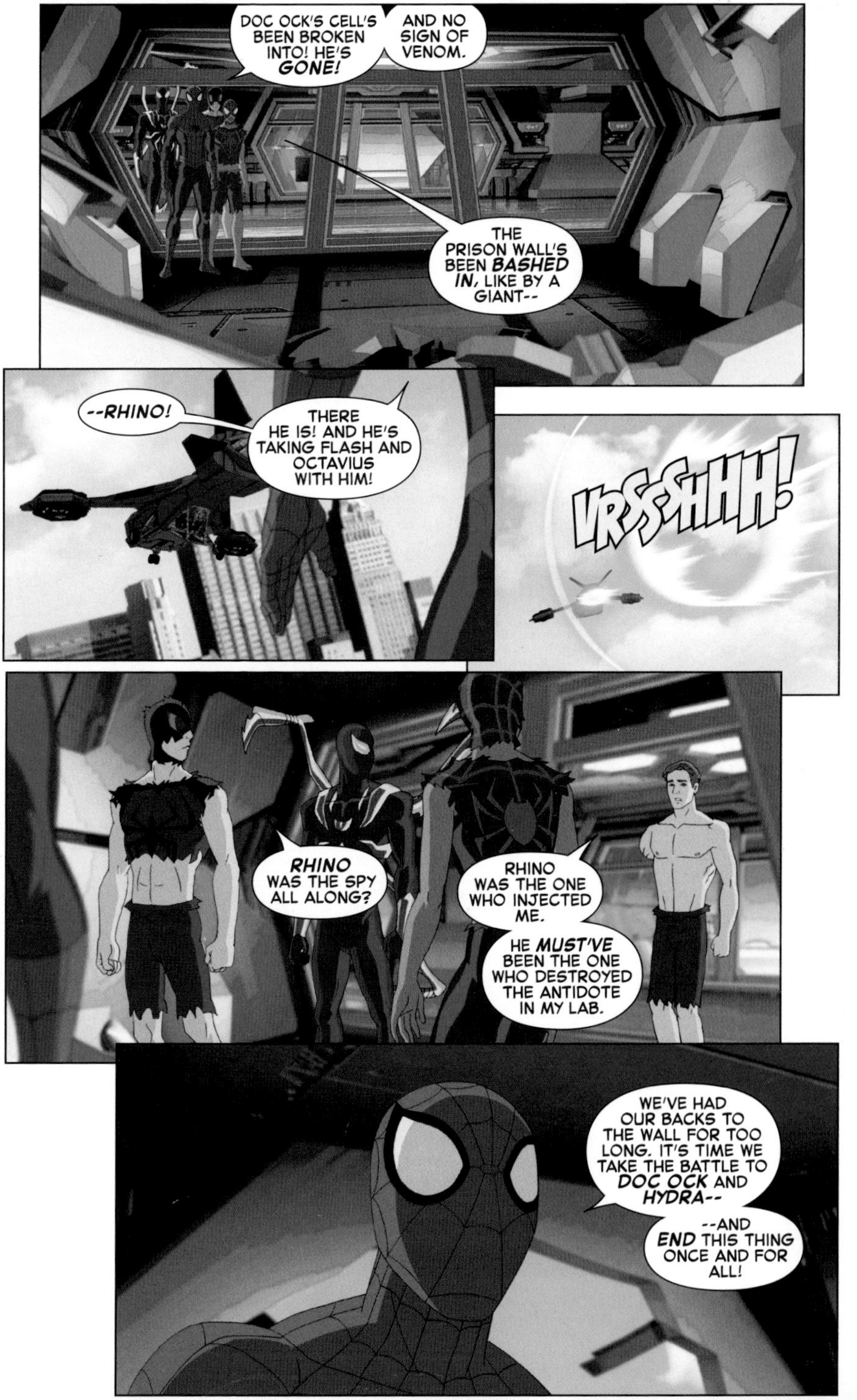
DOC OCK'S CELL'S BEEN BROKEN INTO! HE'S GONE!
AND NO SIGN OF VENOM.
THE PRISON WALL'S BEEN BASHED IN, LIKE BY A GIANT--
--RHINO!
THERE HE IS! AND HE'S TAKING FLASH AND OCTAVIUS WITH HIM!
VRSSHHH!
RHINO WAS THE SPY ALL ALONG?
RHINO WAS THE ONE WHO INJECTED ME.
HE MUST'VE BEEN THE ONE WHO DESTROYED THE ANTIDOTE IN MY LAB.
WE'VE HAD OUR BACKS TO THE WALL FOR TOO LONG. IT'S TIME WE TAKE THE BATTLE TO DOC OCK AND HYDRA--
--AND END THIS THING ONCE AND FOR ALL!

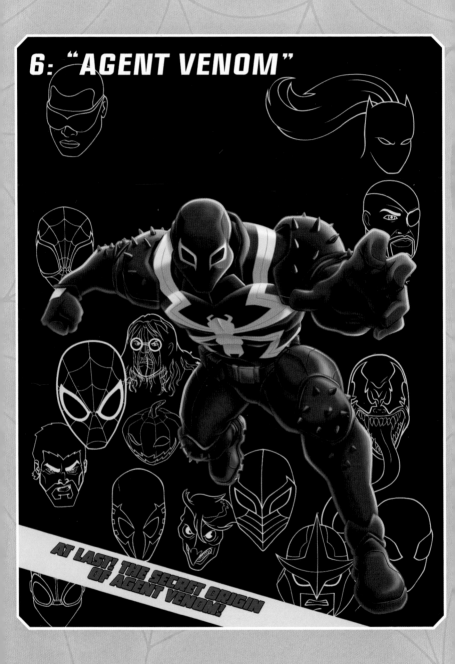

6: "AGENT VENOM"

AT LAST! THE SECRET ORIGIN OF AGENT VENOM!

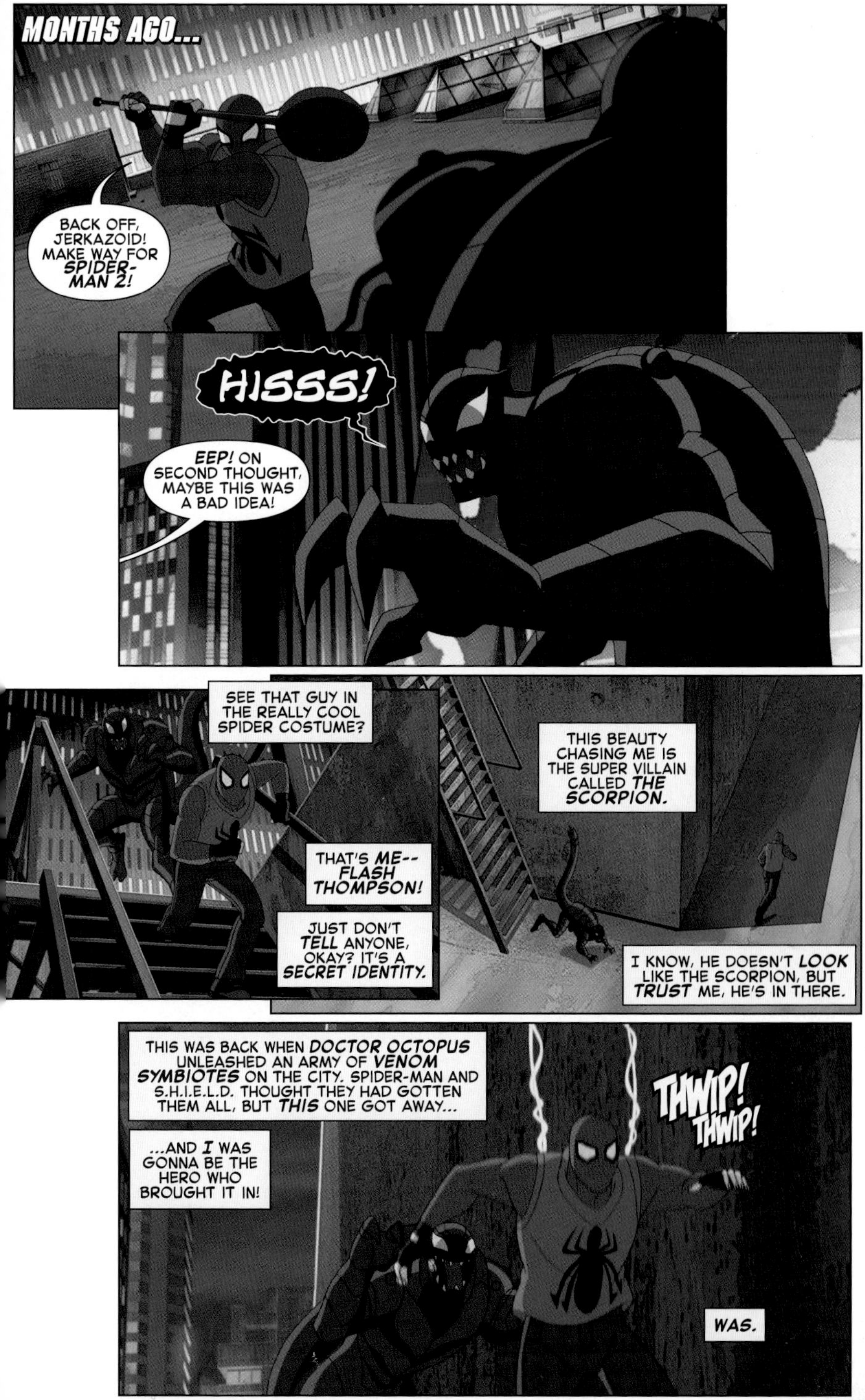
MONTHS AGO...
BACK OFF, JERKAZOID! MAKE WAY FOR SPIDER-MAN 2!
HISSS!
EEP! ON SECOND THOUGHT, MAYBE THIS WAS A BAD IDEA!
SEE THAT GUY IN THE REALLY COOL SPIDER COSTUME?
THAT'S ME--FLASH THOMPSON!
JUST DON'T TELL ANYONE, OKAY? IT'S A SECRET IDENTITY.
THIS BEAUTY CHASING ME IS THE SUPER VILLAIN CALLED THE SCORPION.
I KNOW, HE DOESN'T LOOK LIKE THE SCORPION, BUT TRUST ME, HE'S IN THERE.
THIS WAS BACK WHEN DOCTOR OCTOPUS UNLEASHED AN ARMY OF VENOM SYMBIOTES ON THE CITY. SPIDER-MAN AND S.H.I.E.L.D. THOUGHT THEY HAD GOTTEN THEM ALL, BUT THIS ONE GOT AWAY...
...AND I WAS GONNA BE THE HERO WHO BROUGHT IT IN!
THWIP! THWIP!
WAS.

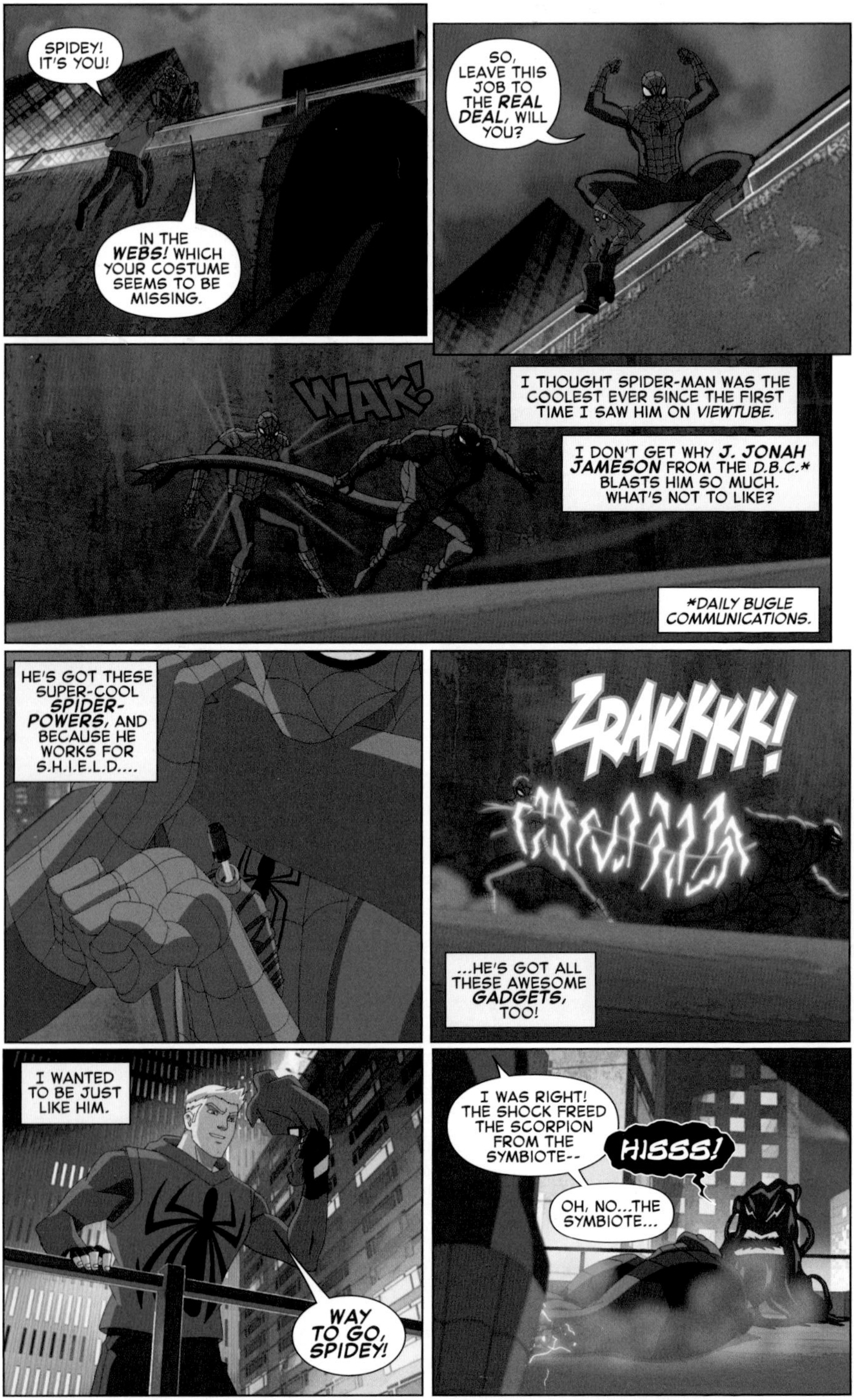
SPIDEY! IT'S YOU!
IN THE WEBS! WHICH YOUR COSTUME SEEMS TO BE MISSING.
SO, LEAVE THIS JOB TO THE REAL DEAL, WILL YOU?
WAK!
I THOUGHT SPIDER-MAN WAS THE COOLEST EVER SINCE THE FIRST TIME I SAW HIM ON VIEWTUBE.
I DON'T GET WHY J. JONAH JAMESON FROM THE D.B.C.* BLASTS HIM SO MUCH. WHAT'S NOT TO LIKE?
*DAILY BUGLE COMMUNICATIONS.
HE'S GOT THESE SUPER-COOL SPIDER-POWERS, AND BECAUSE HE WORKS FOR S.H.I.E.L.D....
ZRAKKKK!
...HE'S GOT ALL THESE AWESOME GADGETS, TOO!
I WANTED TO BE JUST LIKE HIM.
WAY TO GO, SPIDEY!
I WAS RIGHT! THE SHOCK FREED THE SCORPION FROM THE SYMBIOTE--
HISSS!
OH, NO...THE SYMBIOTE...

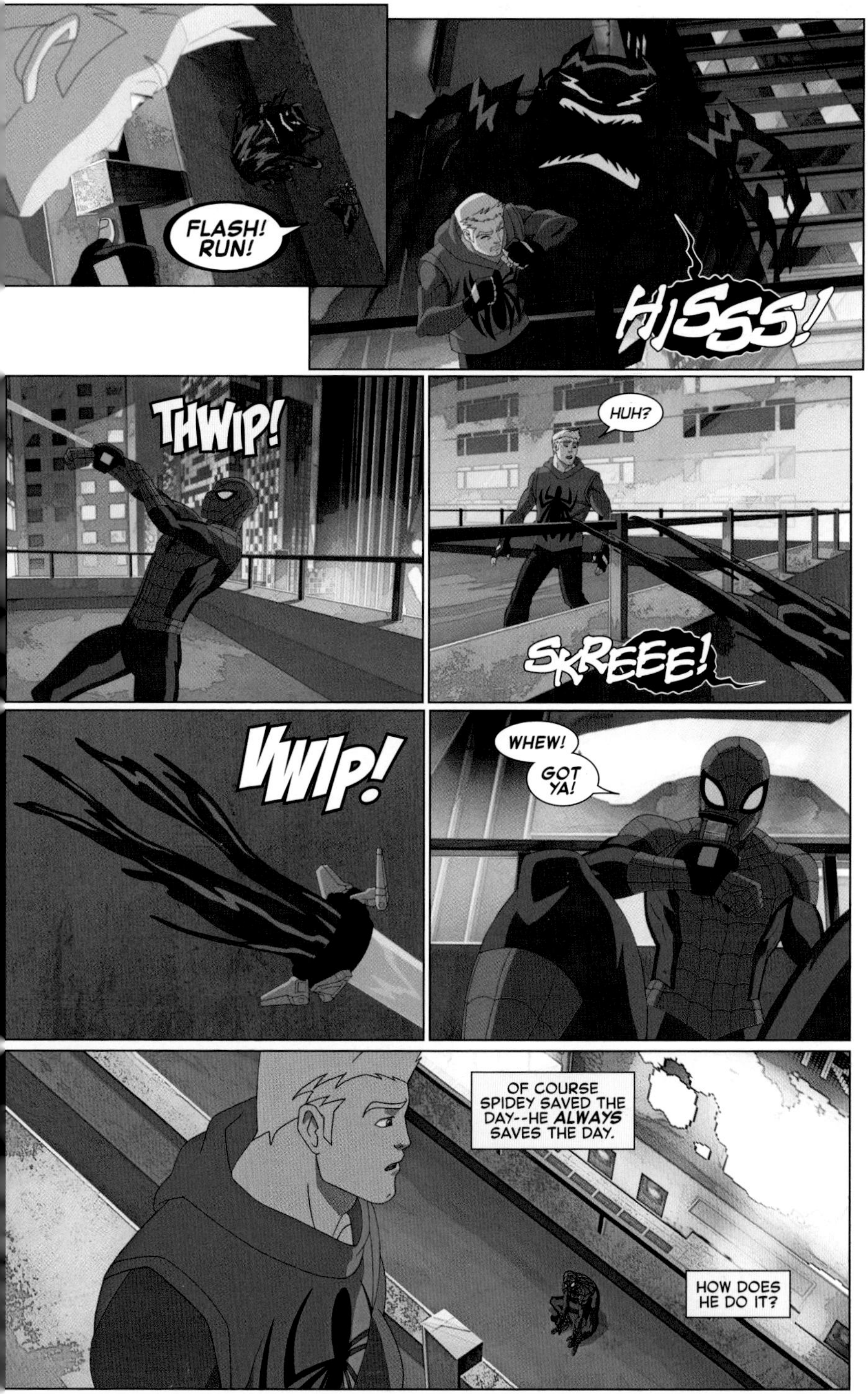
FLASH! RUN!
HISSS!
THWIP!
HUH?
SKREEE!
VWIP!
WHEW!
GOT YA!
OF COURSE SPIDEY SAVED THE DAY--HE *ALWAYS* SAVES THE DAY.
HOW DOES HE DO IT?

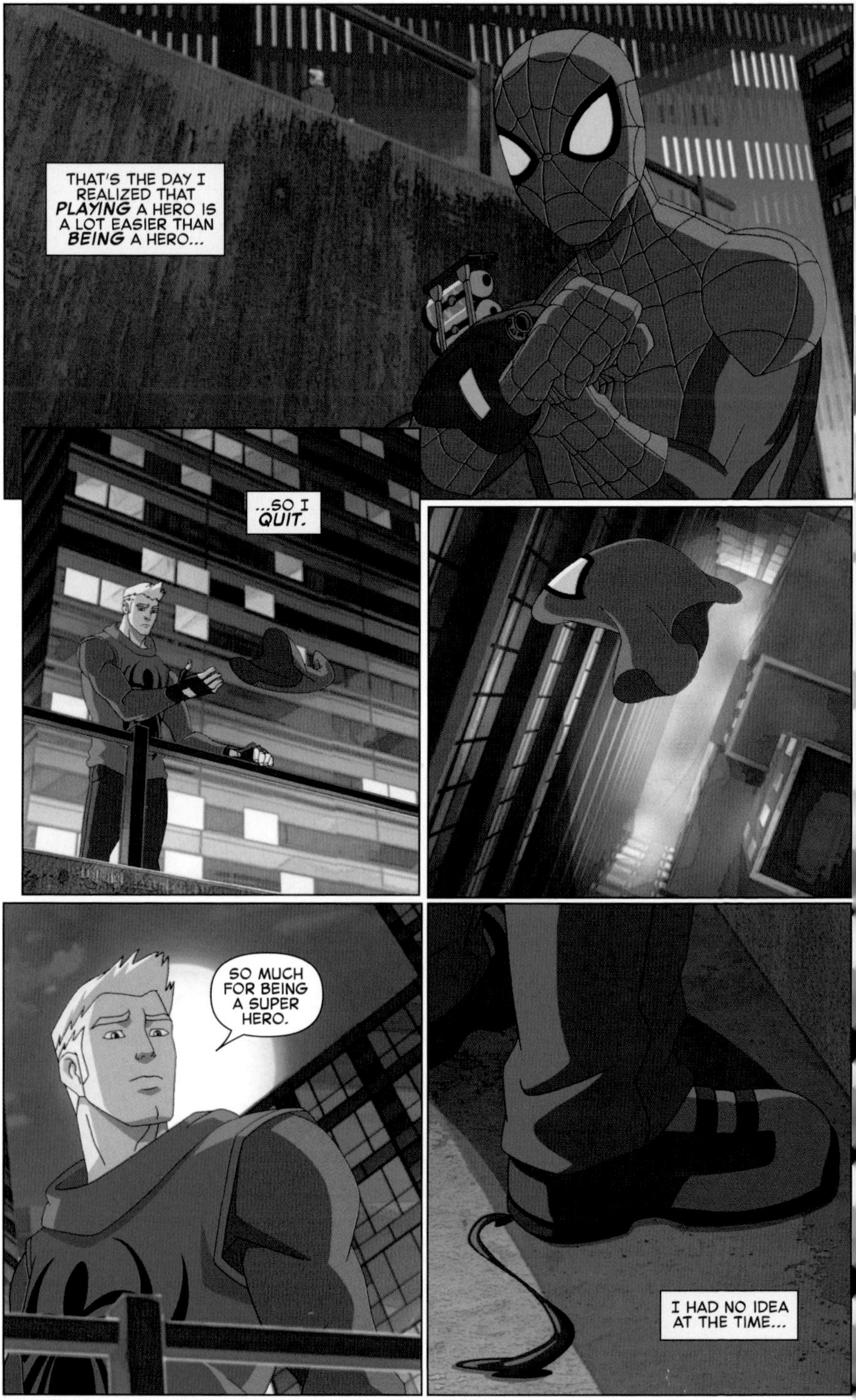
THAT'S THE DAY I REALIZED THAT PLAYING A HERO IS A LOT EASIER THAN BEING A HERO...
...SO I QUIT.
SO MUCH FOR BEING A SUPER HERO.
I HAD NO IDEA AT THE TIME...

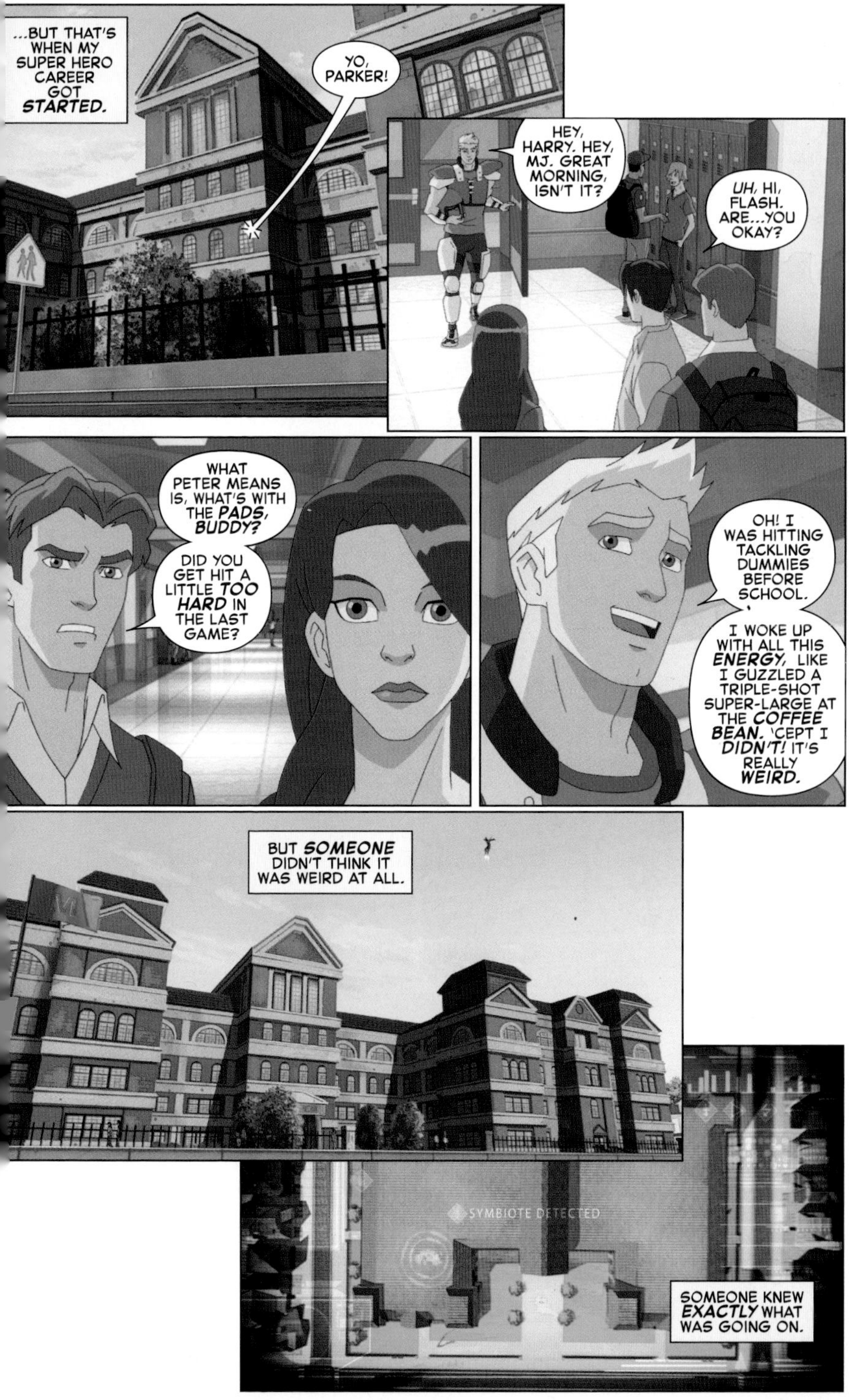
...BUT THAT'S WHEN MY SUPER HERO CAREER GOT STARTED.
YO, PARKER!
HEY, HARRY. HEY, MJ. GREAT MORNING, ISN'T IT?
UH, HI, FLASH. ARE...YOU OKAY?
WHAT PETER MEANS IS, WHAT'S WITH THE PADS, BUDDY?
DID YOU GET HIT A LITTLE TOO HARD IN THE LAST GAME?
OH! I WAS HITTING TACKLING DUMMIES BEFORE SCHOOL.
I WOKE UP WITH ALL THIS ENERGY, LIKE I GUZZLED A TRIPLE-SHOT SUPER-LARGE AT THE COFFEE BEAN. 'CEPT I DIDN'T! IT'S REALLY WEIRD.
BUT SOMEONE DIDN'T THINK IT WAS WEIRD AT ALL.
SYMBIOTE DETECTED
SOMEONE KNEW EXACTLY WHAT WAS GOING ON.

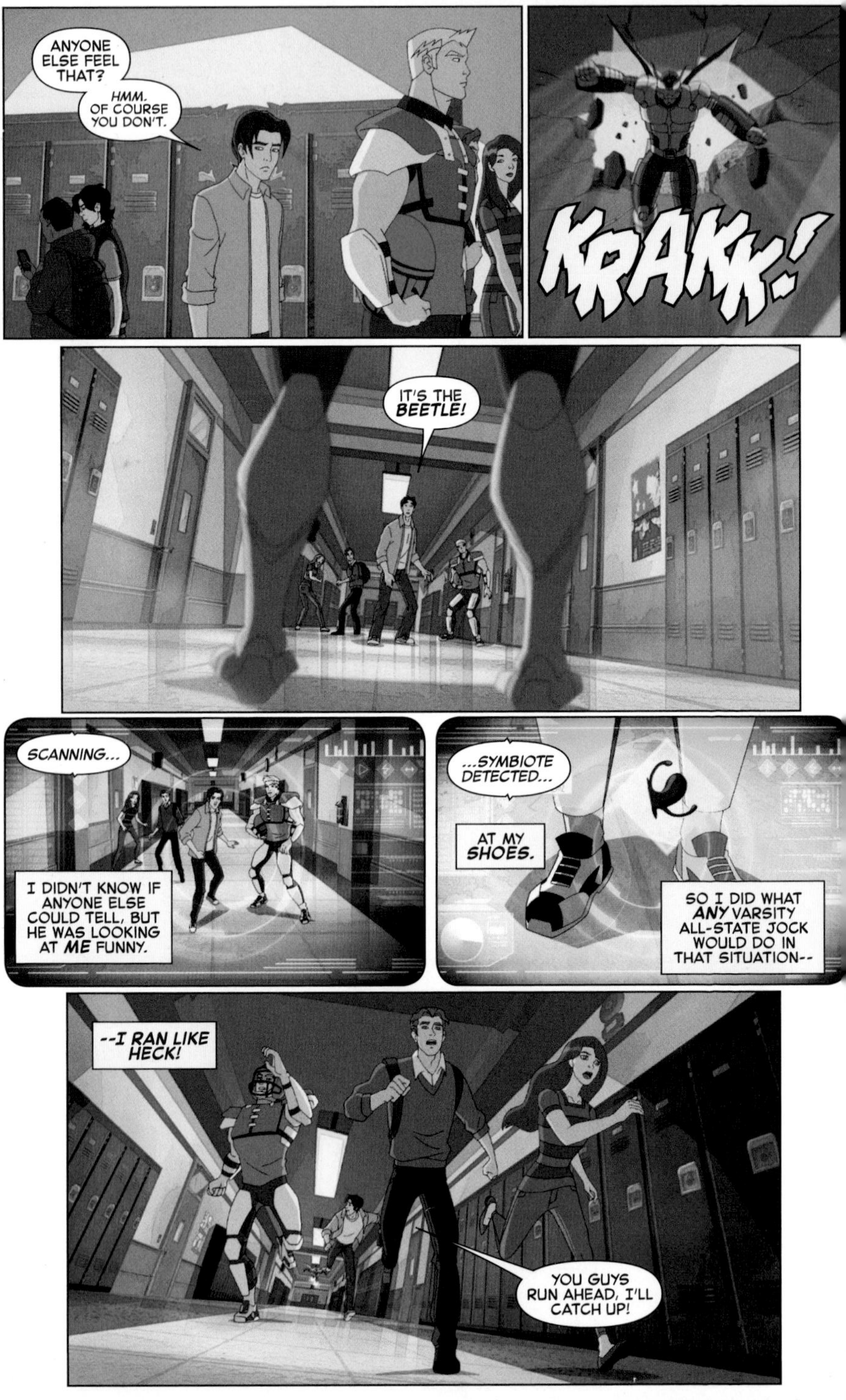
ANYONE ELSE FEEL THAT?
HMM. OF COURSE YOU DON'T.
KRAKK!
IT'S THE BEETLE!
SCANNING...
I DIDN'T KNOW IF ANYONE ELSE COULD TELL, BUT HE WAS LOOKING AT ME FUNNY.
...SYMBIOTE DETECTED...
AT MY SHOES.
SO I DID WHAT ANY VARSITY ALL-STATE JOCK WOULD DO IN THAT SITUATION--
--I RAN LIKE HECK!
YOU GUYS RUN AHEAD, I'LL CATCH UP!

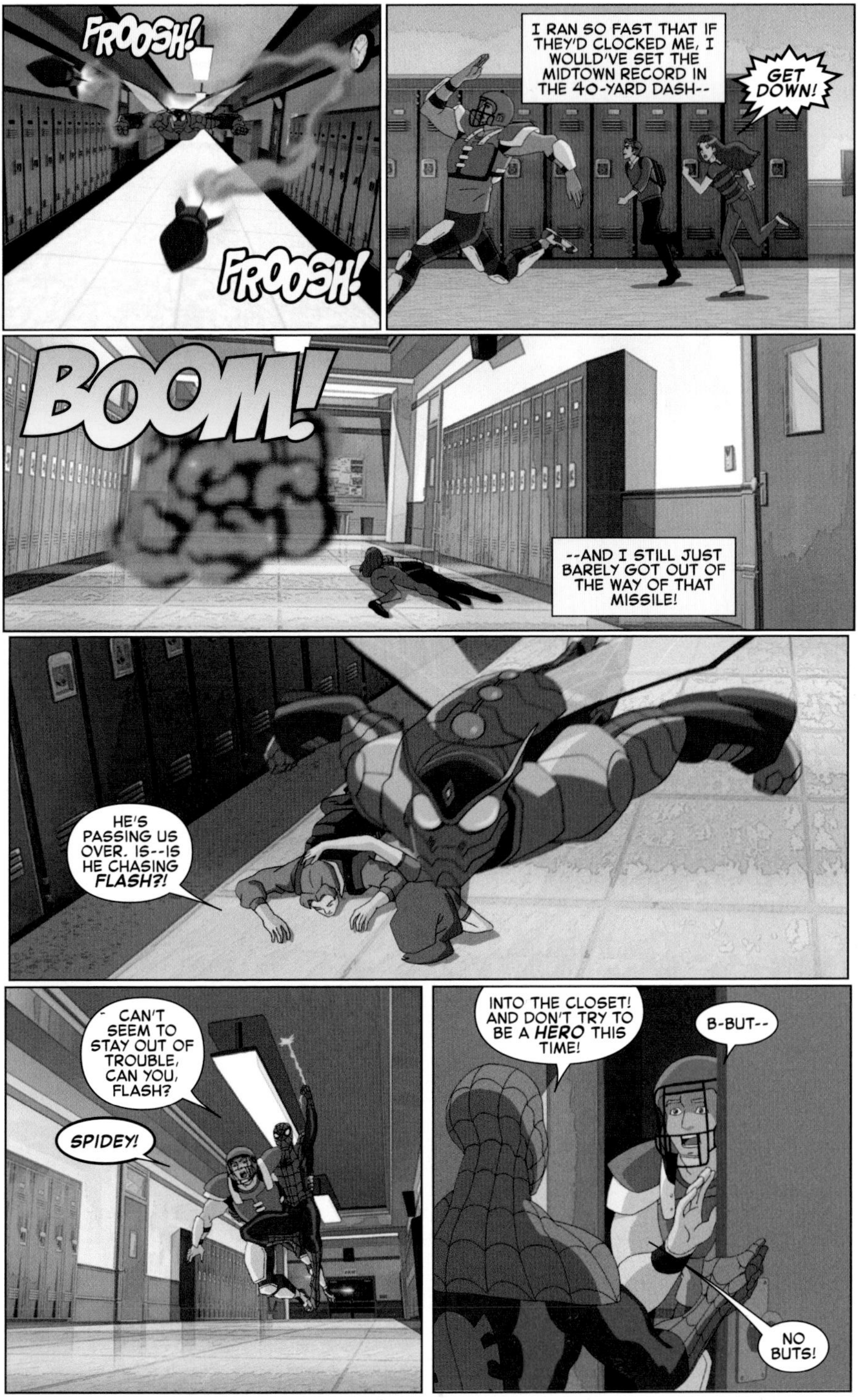
FROOSH!
FROOSH!
I RAN SO FAST THAT IF THEY'D CLOCKED ME, I WOULD'VE SET THE MIDTOWN RECORD IN THE 40-YARD DASH--
GET DOWN!
BOOM!
--AND I STILL JUST BARELY GOT OUT OF THE WAY OF THAT MISSILE!
HE'S PASSING US OVER. IS--IS HE CHASING FLASH?!
CAN'T SEEM TO STAY OUT OF TROUBLE, CAN YOU, FLASH?
SPIDEY!
INTO THE CLOSET! AND DON'T TRY TO BE A HERO THIS TIME!
B-BUT--
NO BUTS!

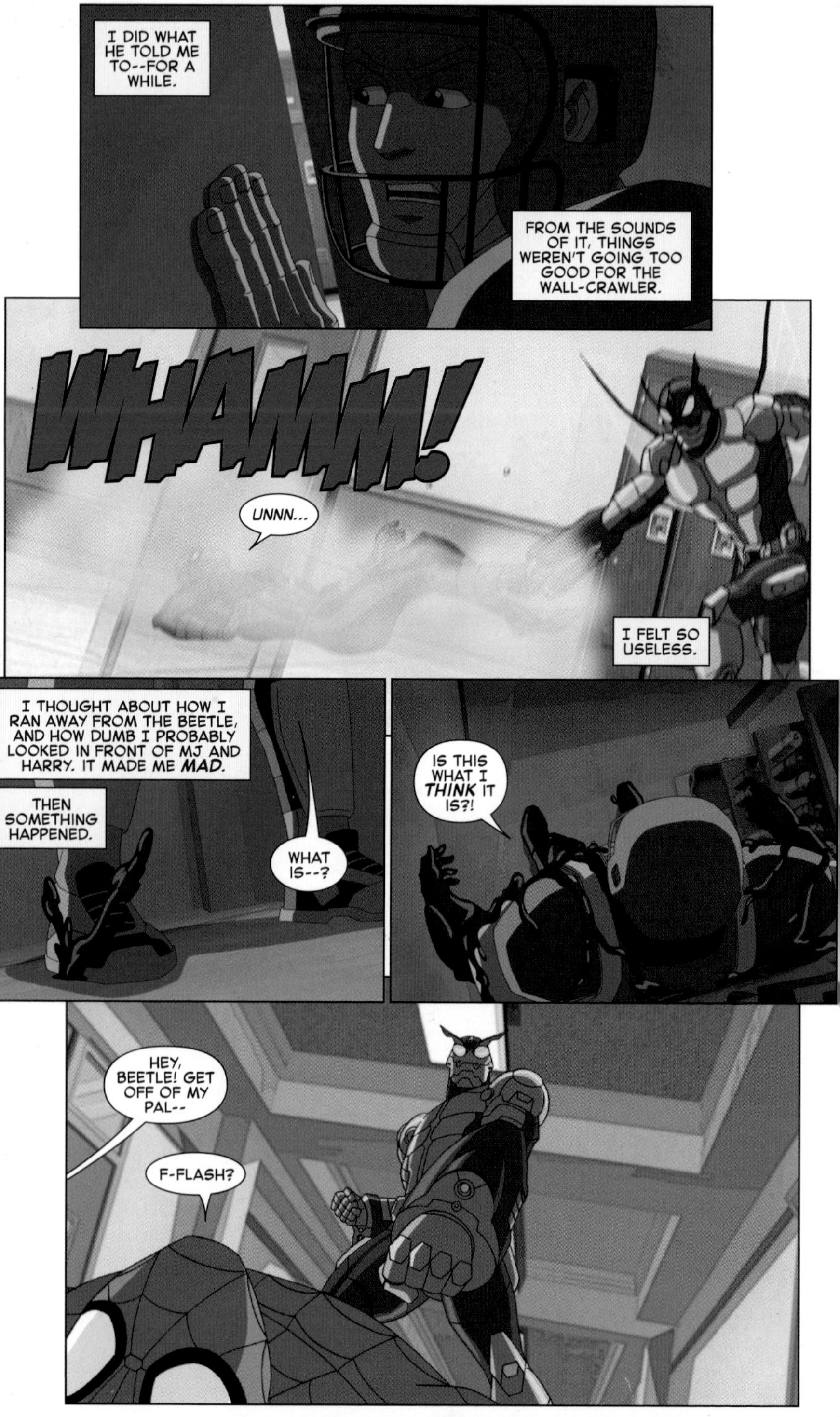
I DID WHAT HE TOLD ME TO--FOR A WHILE.
FROM THE SOUNDS OF IT, THINGS WEREN'T GOING TOO GOOD FOR THE WALL-CRAWLER.
WHAMMM!
UNNN...
I FELT SO USELESS.
I THOUGHT ABOUT HOW I RAN AWAY FROM THE BEETLE, AND HOW DUMB I PROBABLY LOOKED IN FRONT OF MJ AND HARRY. IT MADE ME *MAD.*
THEN SOMETHING HAPPENED.
WHAT IS--?
IS THIS WHAT I *THINK* IT IS?!
HEY, BEETLE! GET OFF OF MY PAL--
F-FLASH?

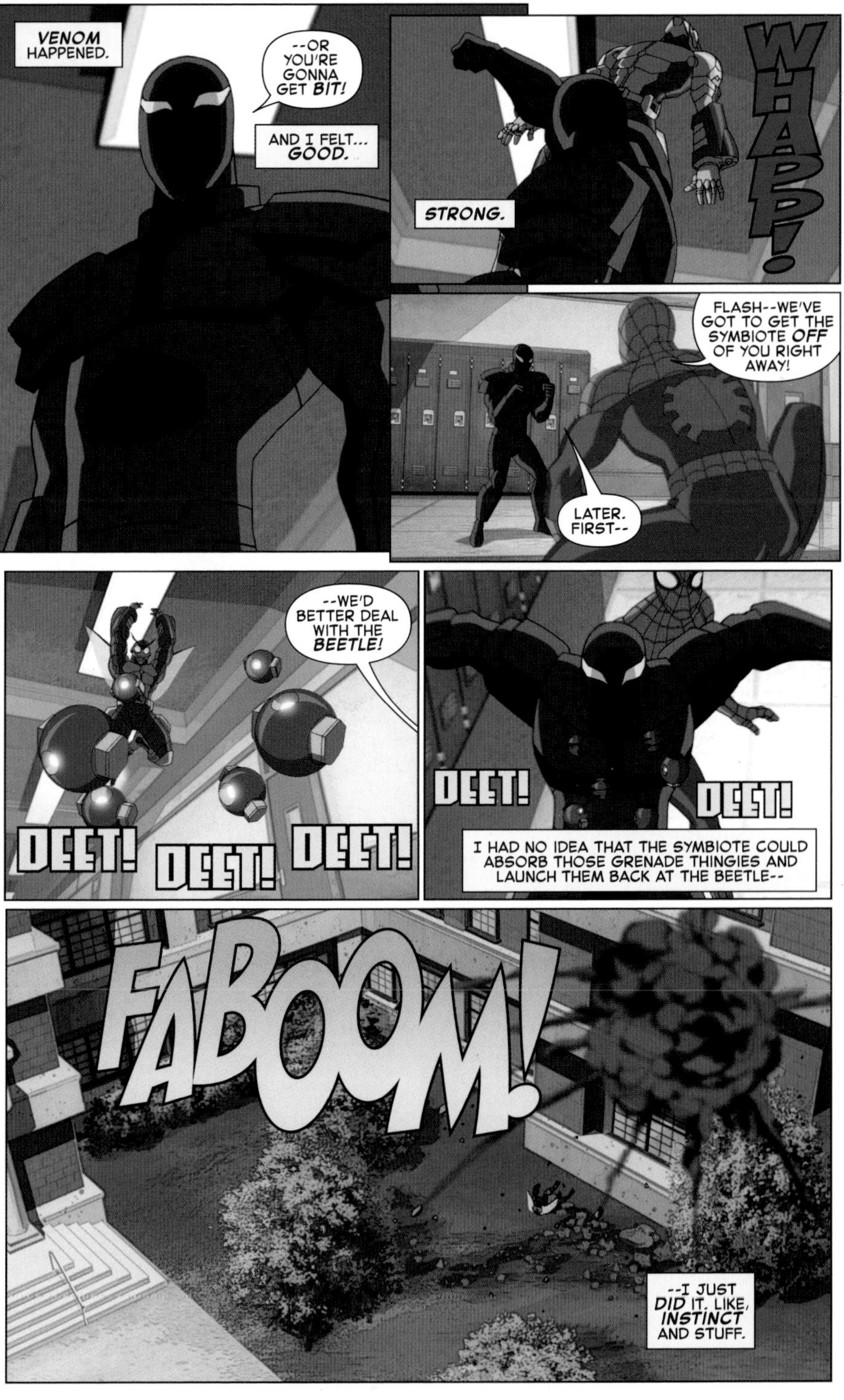
VENOM HAPPENED.
--OR YOU'RE GONNA GET BIT!
AND I FELT... GOOD.
STRONG.
WHAPP!
FLASH--WE'VE GOT TO GET THE SYMBIOTE OFF OF YOU RIGHT AWAY!
LATER. FIRST--
--WE'D BETTER DEAL WITH THE BEETLE!
DEET!
DEET!
DEET!
DEET!
DEET!
I HAD NO IDEA THAT THE SYMBIOTE COULD ABSORB THOSE GRENADE THINGIES AND LAUNCH THEM BACK AT THE BEETLE--
FABOOM!
--I JUST DID IT. LIKE, INSTINCT AND STUFF.

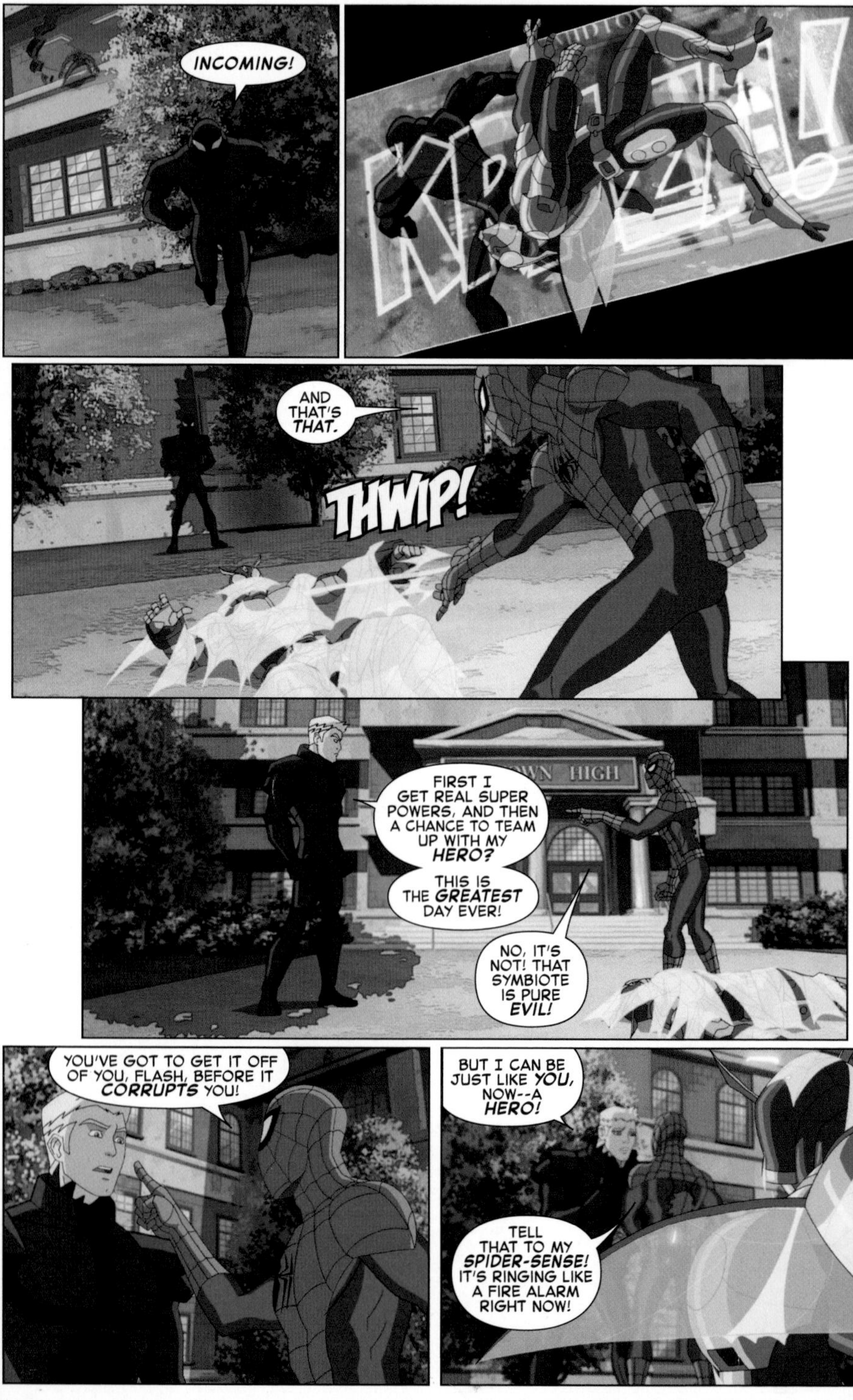

INCOMING!
AND THAT'S THAT.
THWIP!
FIRST I GET REAL SUPER POWERS, AND THEN A CHANCE TO TEAM UP WITH MY HERO?
THIS IS THE GREATEST DAY EVER!
NO, IT'S NOT! THAT SYMBIOTE IS PURE EVIL!
YOU'VE GOT TO GET IT OFF OF YOU, FLASH, BEFORE IT CORRUPTS YOU!
BUT I CAN BE JUST LIKE YOU, NOW--A HERO!
TELL THAT TO MY SPIDER-SENSE! IT'S RINGING LIKE A FIRE ALARM RIGHT NOW!

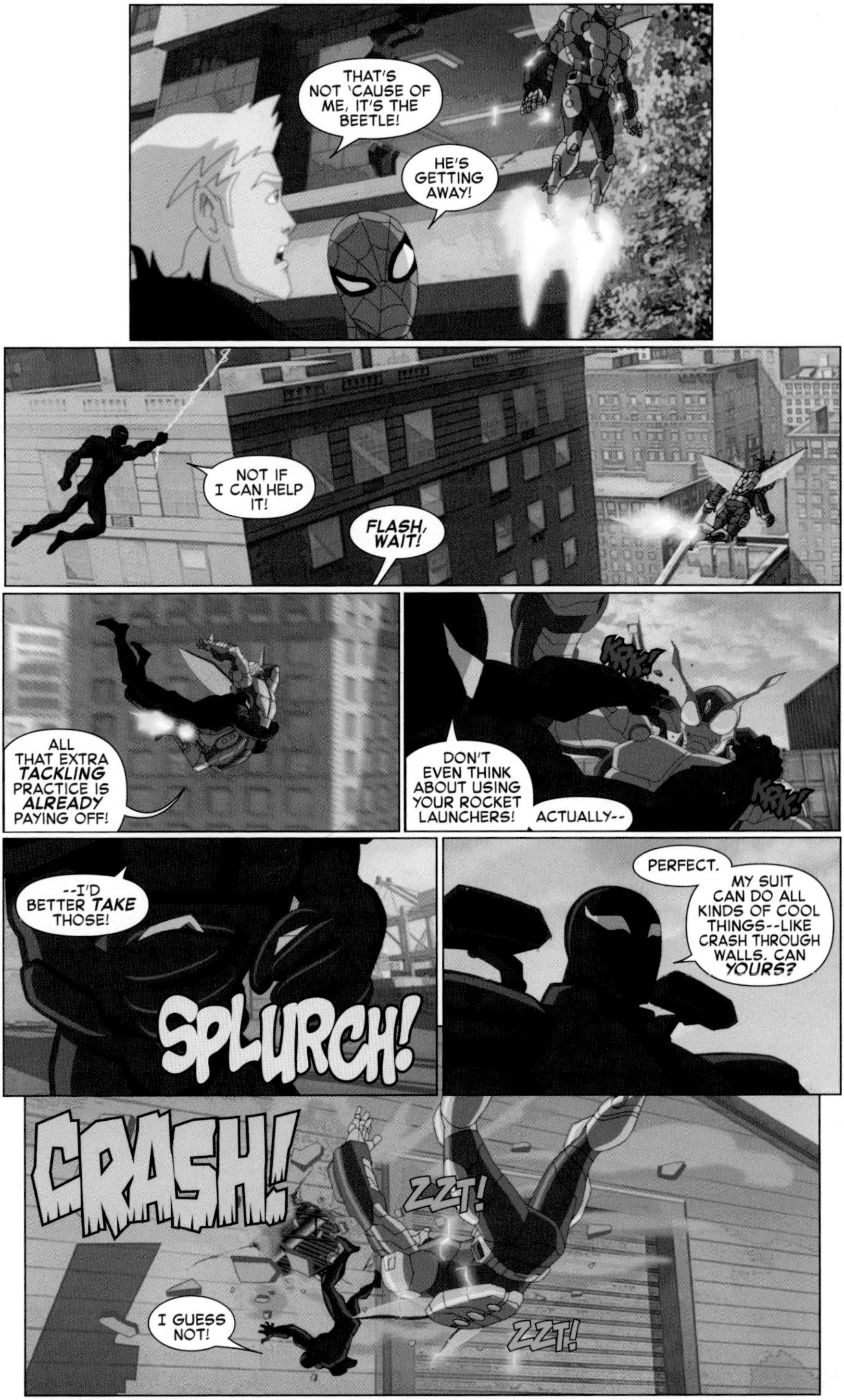
THAT'S NOT 'CAUSE OF ME, IT'S THE BEETLE!
HE'S GETTING AWAY!
NOT IF I CAN HELP IT!
FLASH, WAIT!
ALL THAT EXTRA TACKLING PRACTICE IS ALREADY PAYING OFF!
KRK!
DON'T EVEN THINK ABOUT USING YOUR ROCKET LAUNCHERS!
ACTUALLY--
KRK!
--I'D BETTER TAKE THOSE!
SPLURCH!
PERFECT.
MY SUIT CAN DO ALL KINDS OF COOL THINGS--LIKE CRASH THROUGH WALLS. CAN YOURS?
CRASH!
ZZT!
I GUESS NOT!
ZZT!

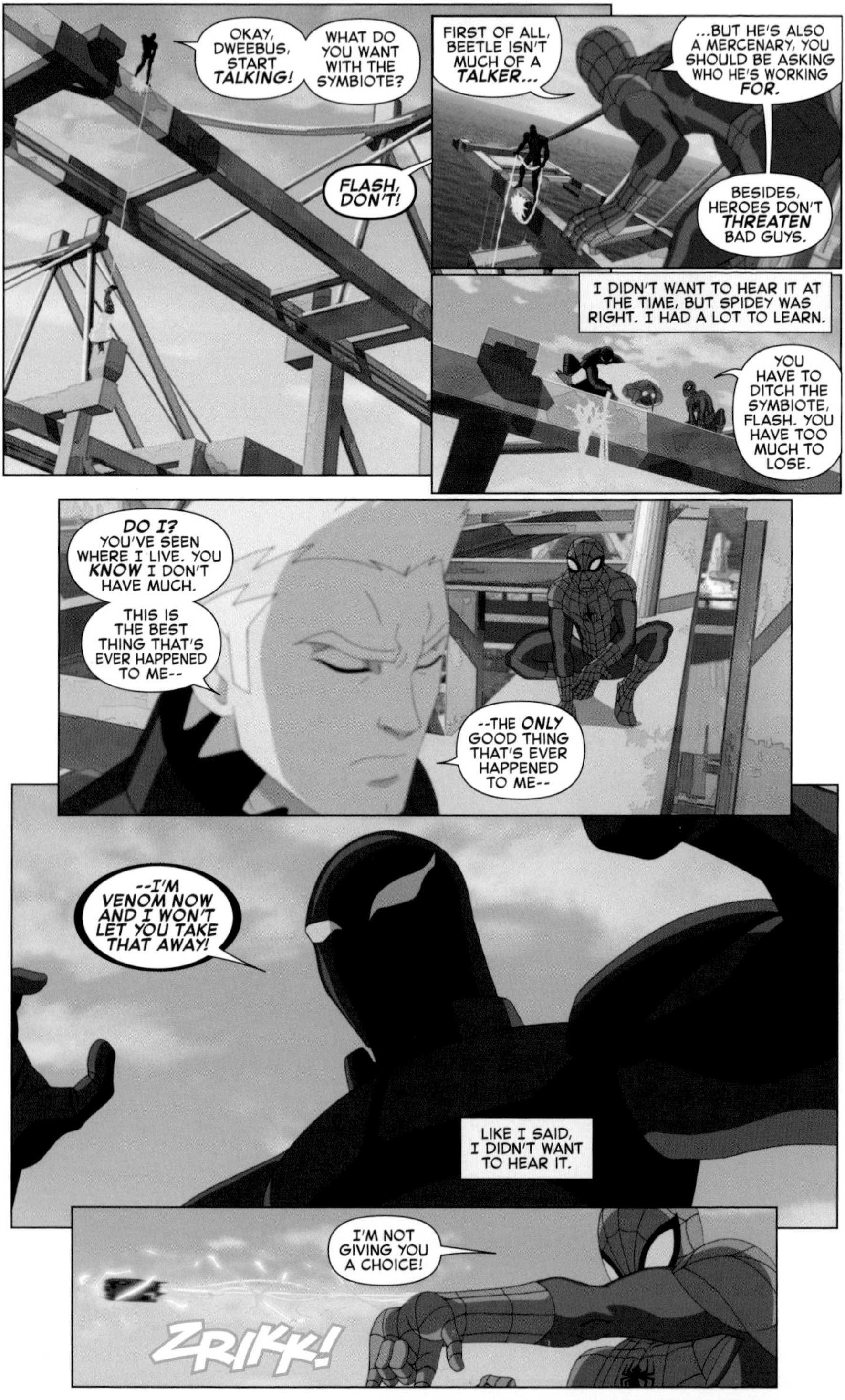
OKAY, DWEEBUS, START TALKING!
WHAT DO YOU WANT WITH THE SYMBIOTE?
FLASH, DON'T!
FIRST OF ALL, BEETLE ISN'T MUCH OF A TALKER...
...BUT HE'S ALSO A MERCENARY, YOU SHOULD BE ASKING WHO HE'S WORKING FOR.
BESIDES, HEROES DON'T THREATEN BAD GUYS.
I DIDN'T WANT TO HEAR IT AT THE TIME, BUT SPIDEY WAS RIGHT. I HAD A LOT TO LEARN.
YOU HAVE TO DITCH THE SYMBIOTE, FLASH. YOU HAVE TOO MUCH TO LOSE.
DO I? YOU'VE SEEN WHERE I LIVE. YOU KNOW I DON'T HAVE MUCH.
THIS IS THE BEST THING THAT'S EVER HAPPENED TO ME--
--THE ONLY GOOD THING THAT'S EVER HAPPENED TO ME--
--I'M VENOM NOW AND I WON'T LET YOU TAKE THAT AWAY!
LIKE I SAID, I DIDN'T WANT TO HEAR IT.
I'M NOT GIVING YOU A CHOICE!
ZRIKK!

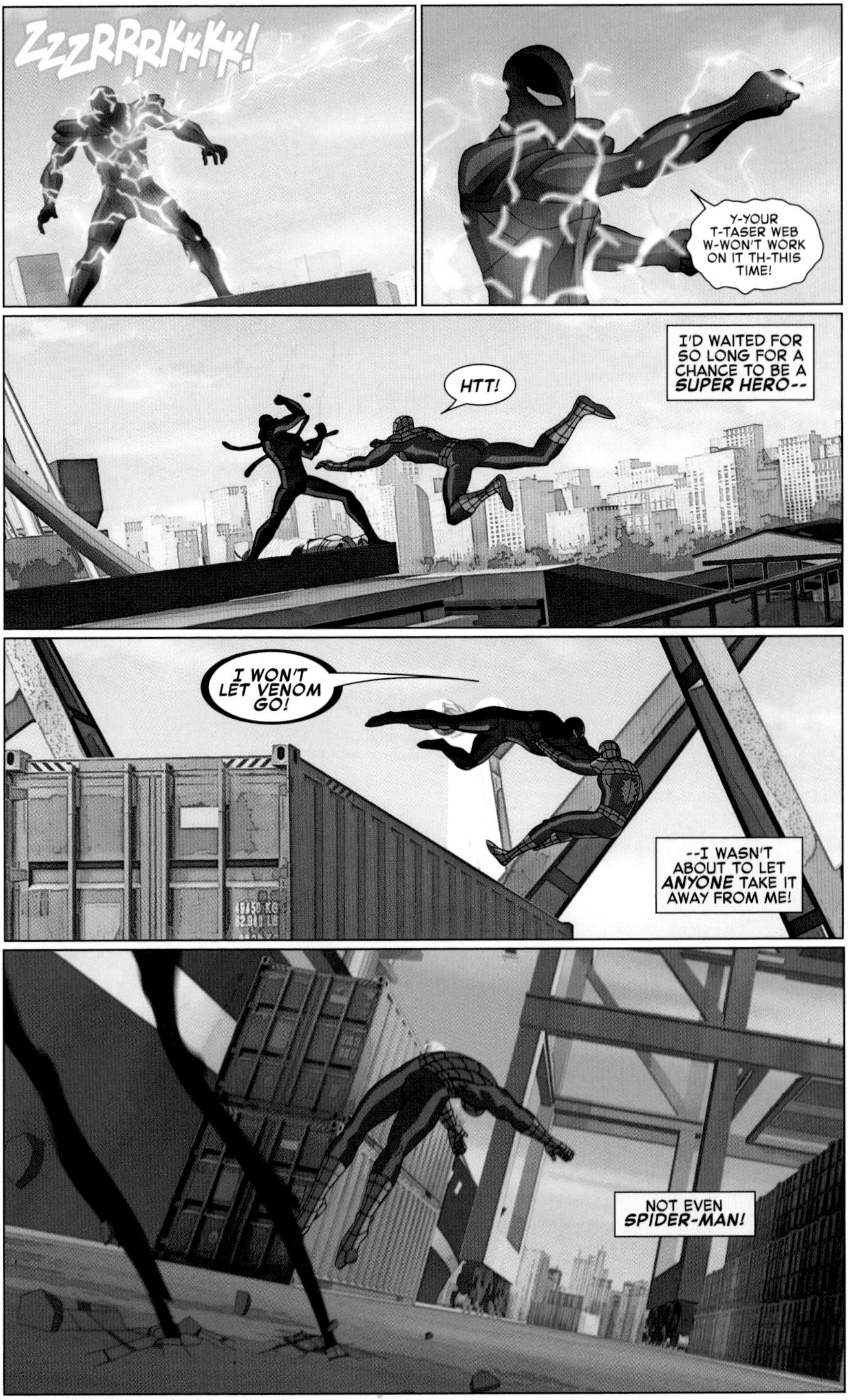
ZZZRRRKKKK!
Y-YOUR T-TASER WEB W-WON'T WORK ON IT TH-THIS TIME!
I'D WAITED FOR SO LONG FOR A CHANCE TO BE A SUPER HERO--
HTT!
I WON'T LET VENOM GO!
--I WASN'T ABOUT TO LET ANYONE TAKE IT AWAY FROM ME!
NOT EVEN SPIDER-MAN!

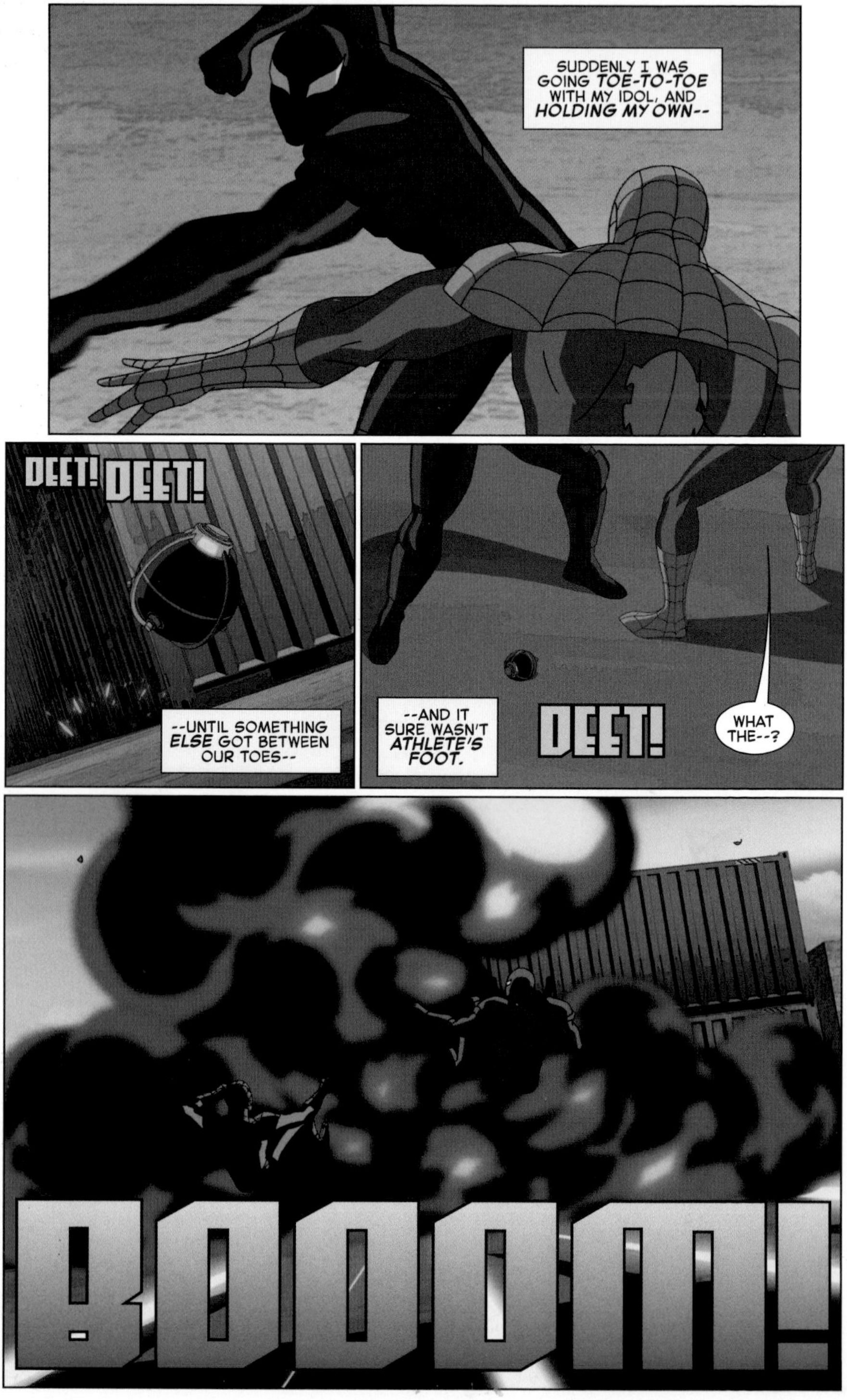
SUDDENLY I WAS GOING TOE-TO-TOE WITH MY IDOL, AND HOLDING MY OWN--
DEET! DEET!
--UNTIL SOMETHING ELSE GOT BETWEEN OUR TOES--
--AND IT SURE WASN'T ATHLETE'S FOOT.
DEET!
WHAT THE--?
BOOM!

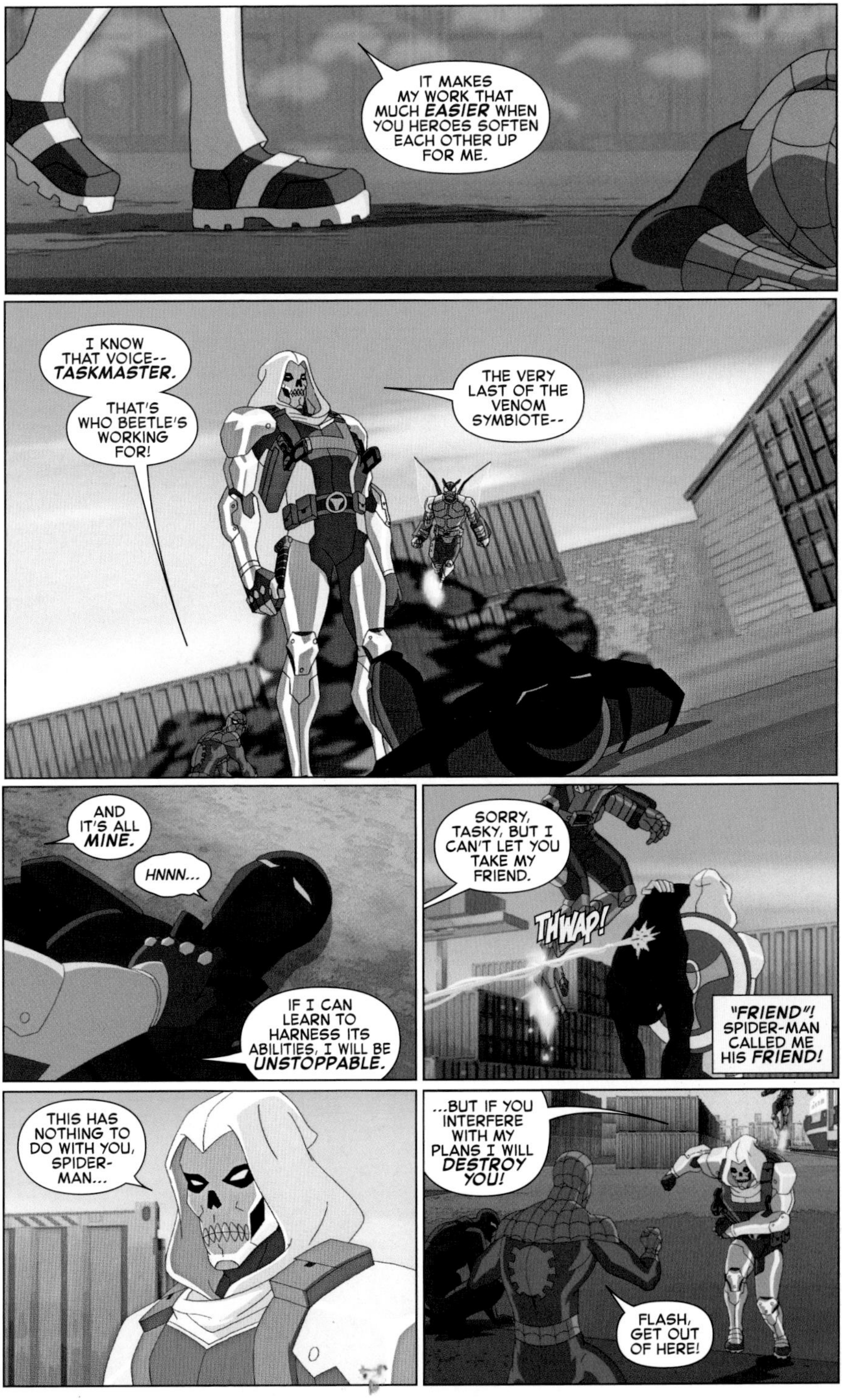
IT MAKES MY WORK THAT MUCH EASIER WHEN YOU HEROES SOFTEN EACH OTHER UP FOR ME.
I KNOW THAT VOICE-- TASKMASTER.
THAT'S WHO BEETLE'S WORKING FOR!
THE VERY LAST OF THE VENOM SYMBIOTE--
AND IT'S ALL MINE.
HNNN...
IF I CAN LEARN TO HARNESS ITS ABILITIES, I WILL BE UNSTOPPABLE.
SORRY, TASKY, BUT I CAN'T LET YOU TAKE MY FRIEND.
THWAP!
"FRIEND"! SPIDER-MAN CALLED ME HIS FRIEND!
THIS HAS NOTHING TO DO WITH YOU, SPIDER-MAN...
...BUT IF YOU INTERFERE WITH MY PLANS I WILL DESTROY YOU!
FLASH, GET OUT OF HERE!

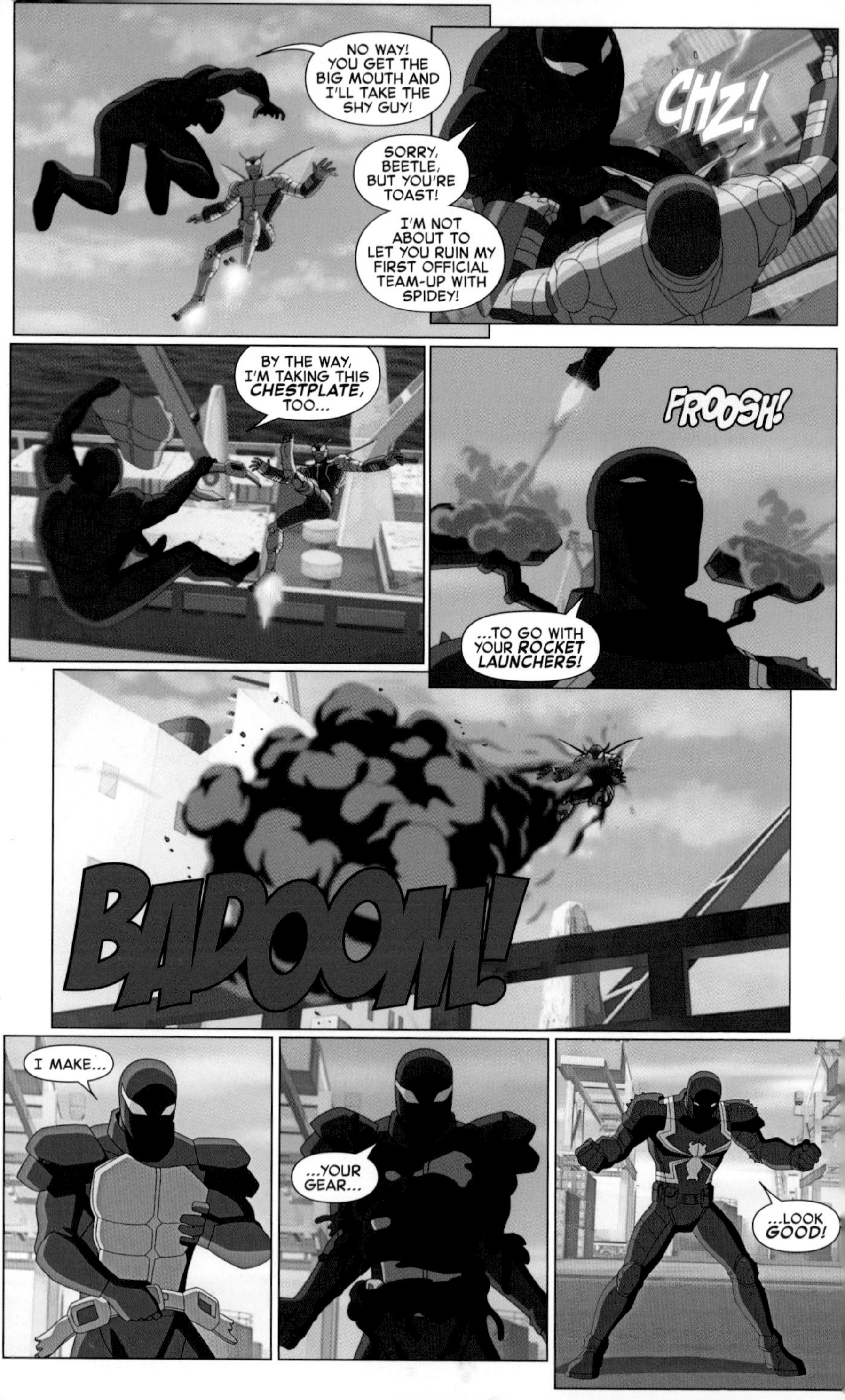
NO WAY! YOU GET THE BIG MOUTH AND I'LL TAKE THE SHY GUY!
CHZ!
SORRY, BEETLE, BUT YOU'RE TOAST!
I'M NOT ABOUT TO LET YOU RUIN MY FIRST OFFICIAL TEAM-UP WITH SPIDEY!
BY THE WAY, I'M TAKING THIS CHESTPLATE, TOO...
FROOSH!
...TO GO WITH YOUR ROCKET LAUNCHERS!
BADOOM!
I MAKE...
...YOUR GEAR...
...LOOK GOOD!

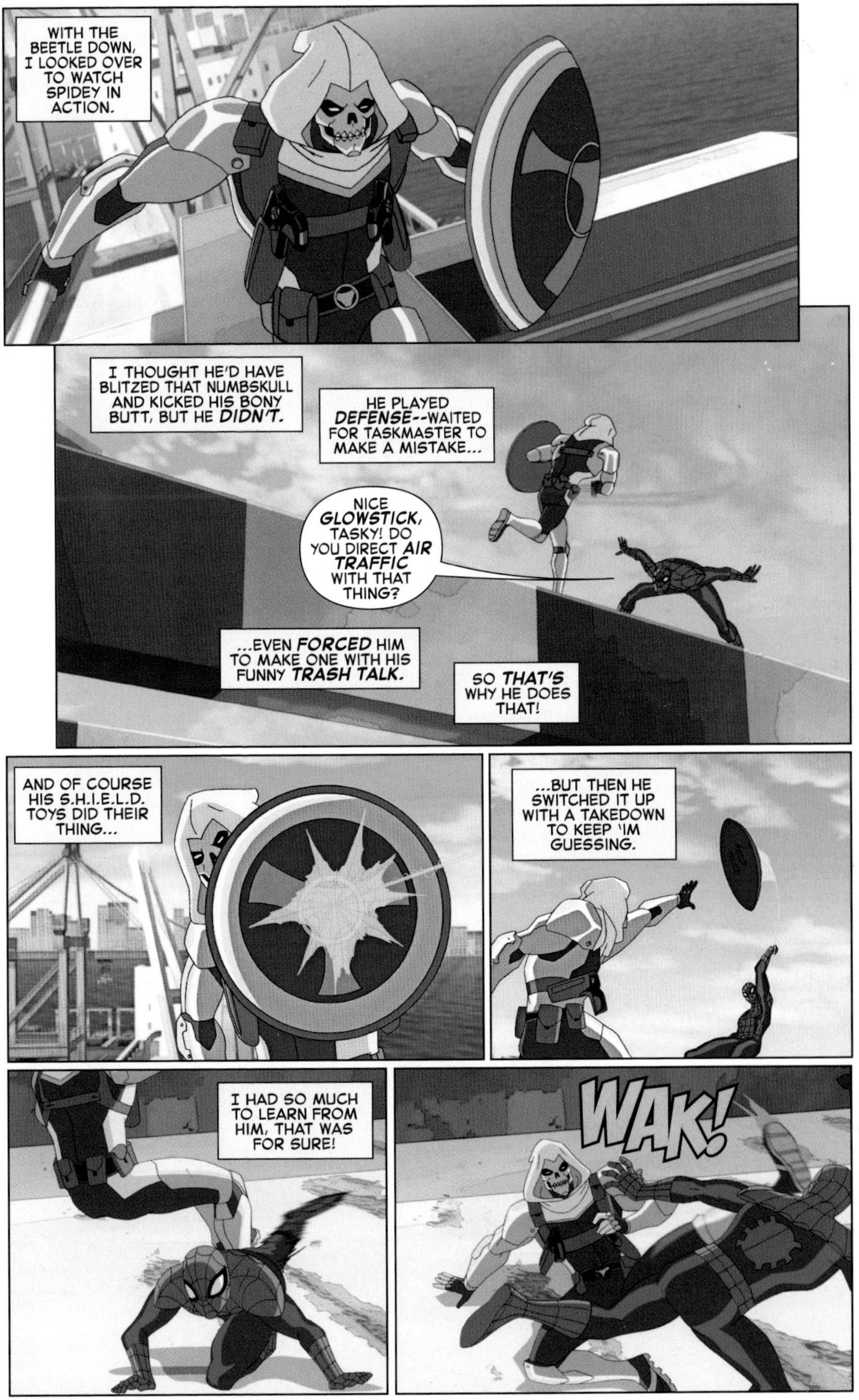
WITH THE BEETLE DOWN, I LOOKED OVER TO WATCH SPIDEY IN ACTION.
I THOUGHT HE'D HAVE BLITZED THAT NUMBSKULL AND KICKED HIS BONY BUTT, BUT HE DIDN'T.
HE PLAYED DEFENSE--WAITED FOR TASKMASTER TO MAKE A MISTAKE...
NICE GLOWSTICK, TASKY! DO YOU DIRECT AIR TRAFFIC WITH THAT THING?
...EVEN FORCED HIM TO MAKE ONE WITH HIS FUNNY TRASH TALK.
SO THAT'S WHY HE DOES THAT!
AND OF COURSE HIS S.H.I.E.L.D. TOYS DID THEIR THING...
...BUT THEN HE SWITCHED IT UP WITH A TAKEDOWN TO KEEP 'IM GUESSING.
I HAD SO MUCH TO LEARN FROM HIM, THAT WAS FOR SURE!
WAK!

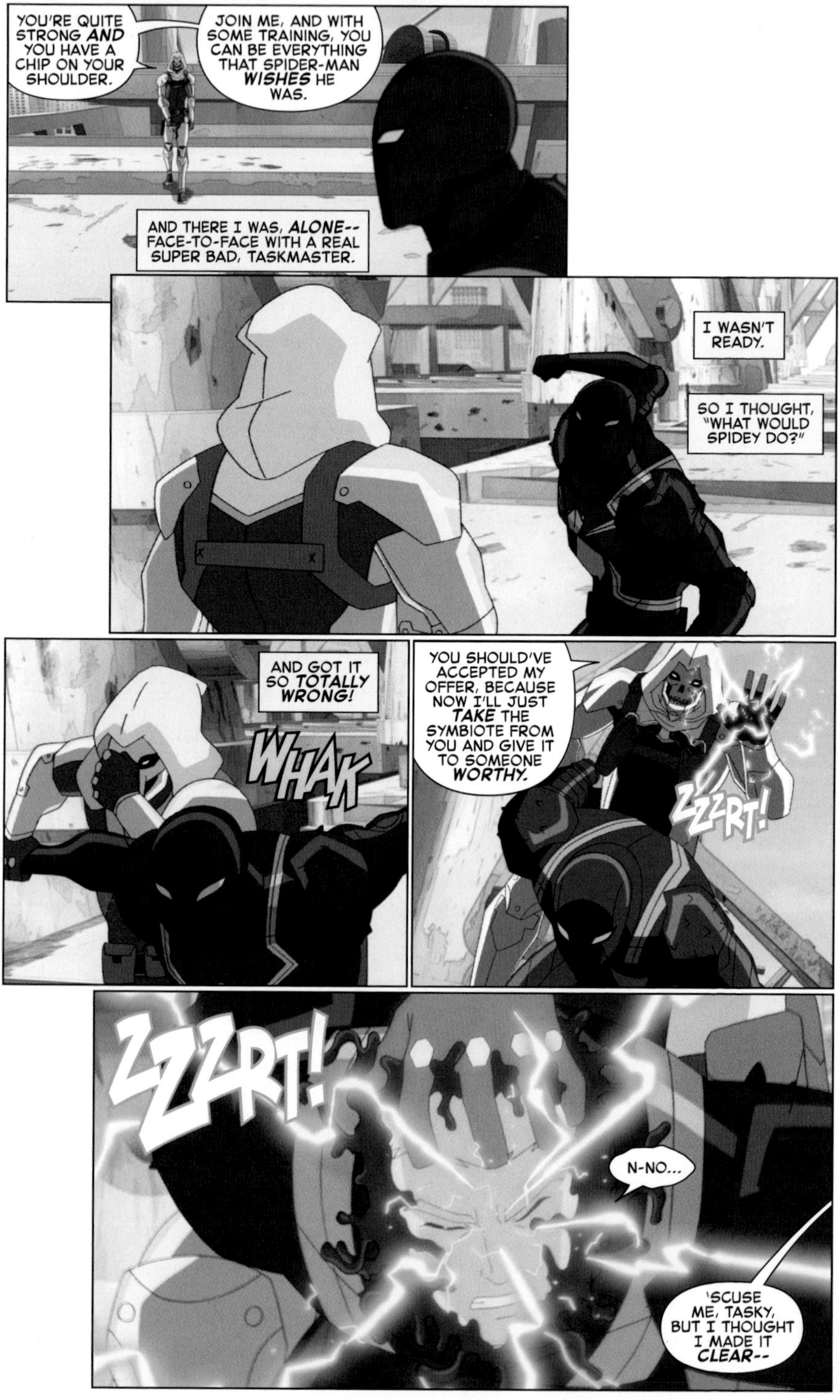
YOU'RE QUITE STRONG AND YOU HAVE A CHIP ON YOUR SHOULDER.
JOIN ME, AND WITH SOME TRAINING, YOU CAN BE EVERYTHING THAT SPIDER-MAN WISHES HE WAS.
AND THERE I WAS, ALONE--FACE-TO-FACE WITH A REAL SUPER BAD, TASKMASTER.
I WASN'T READY.
SO I THOUGHT, "WHAT WOULD SPIDEY DO?"
AND GOT IT SO TOTALLY WRONG!
WHAK
YOU SHOULD'VE ACCEPTED MY OFFER, BECAUSE NOW I'LL JUST TAKE THE SYMBIOTE FROM YOU AND GIVE IT TO SOMEONE WORTHY.
ZZZRT!
ZZZRT!
N-NO...
'SCUSE ME, TASKY, BUT I THOUGHT I MADE IT CLEAR--

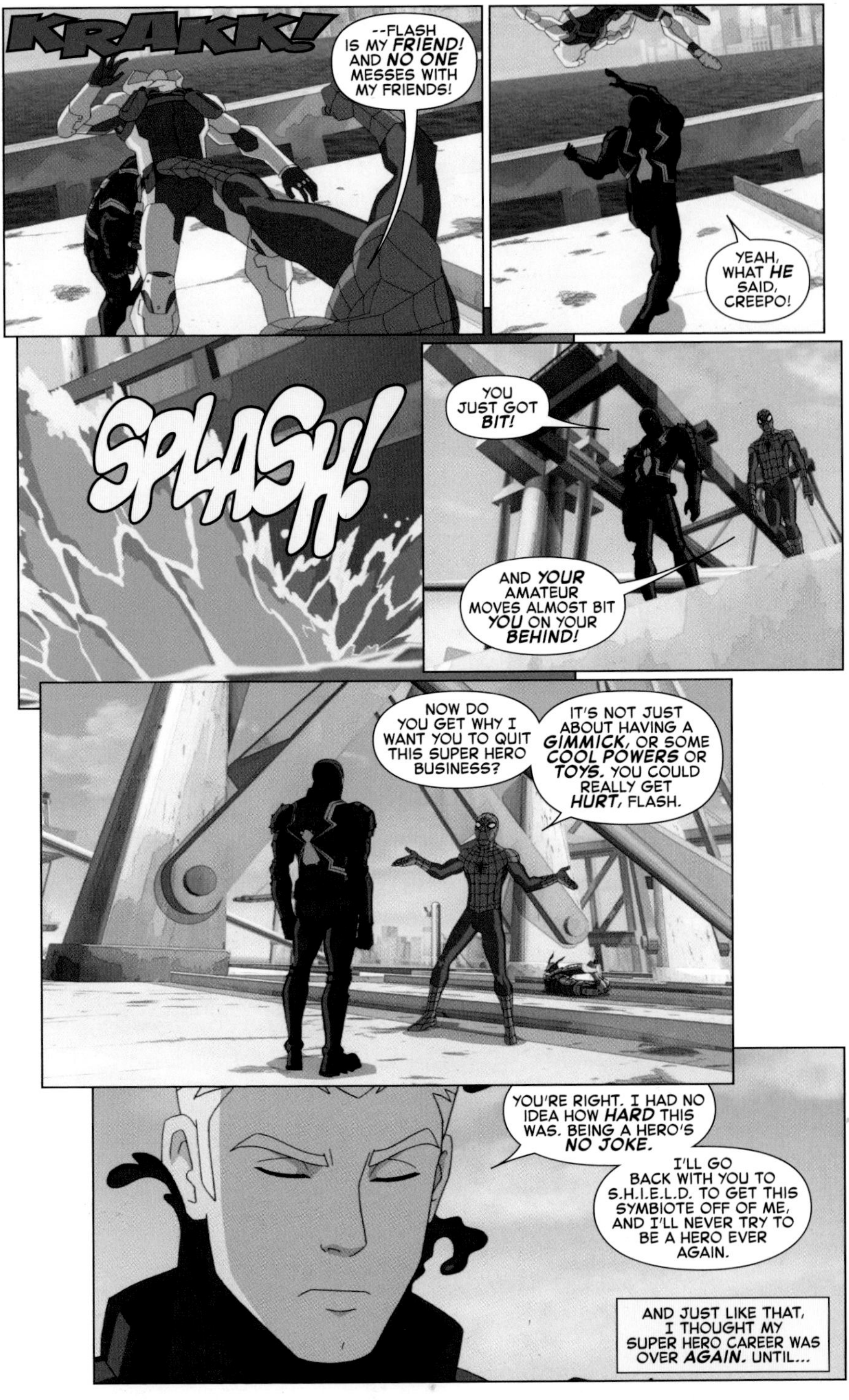
KRAKK!
--FLASH IS MY FRIEND! AND NO ONE MESSES WITH MY FRIENDS!
YEAH, WHAT HE SAID, CREEPO!
SPLASH!
YOU JUST GOT BIT!
AND YOUR AMATEUR MOVES ALMOST BIT YOU ON YOUR BEHIND!
NOW DO YOU GET WHY I WANT YOU TO QUIT THIS SUPER HERO BUSINESS?
IT'S NOT JUST ABOUT HAVING A GIMMICK, OR SOME COOL POWERS OR TOYS. YOU COULD REALLY GET HURT, FLASH.
YOU'RE RIGHT. I HAD NO IDEA HOW HARD THIS WAS. BEING A HERO'S NO JOKE.
I'LL GO BACK WITH YOU TO S.H.I.E.L.D. TO GET THIS SYMBIOTE OFF OF ME, AND I'LL NEVER TRY TO BE A HERO EVER AGAIN.
AND JUST LIKE THAT, I THOUGHT MY SUPER HERO CAREER WAS OVER AGAIN. UNTIL...

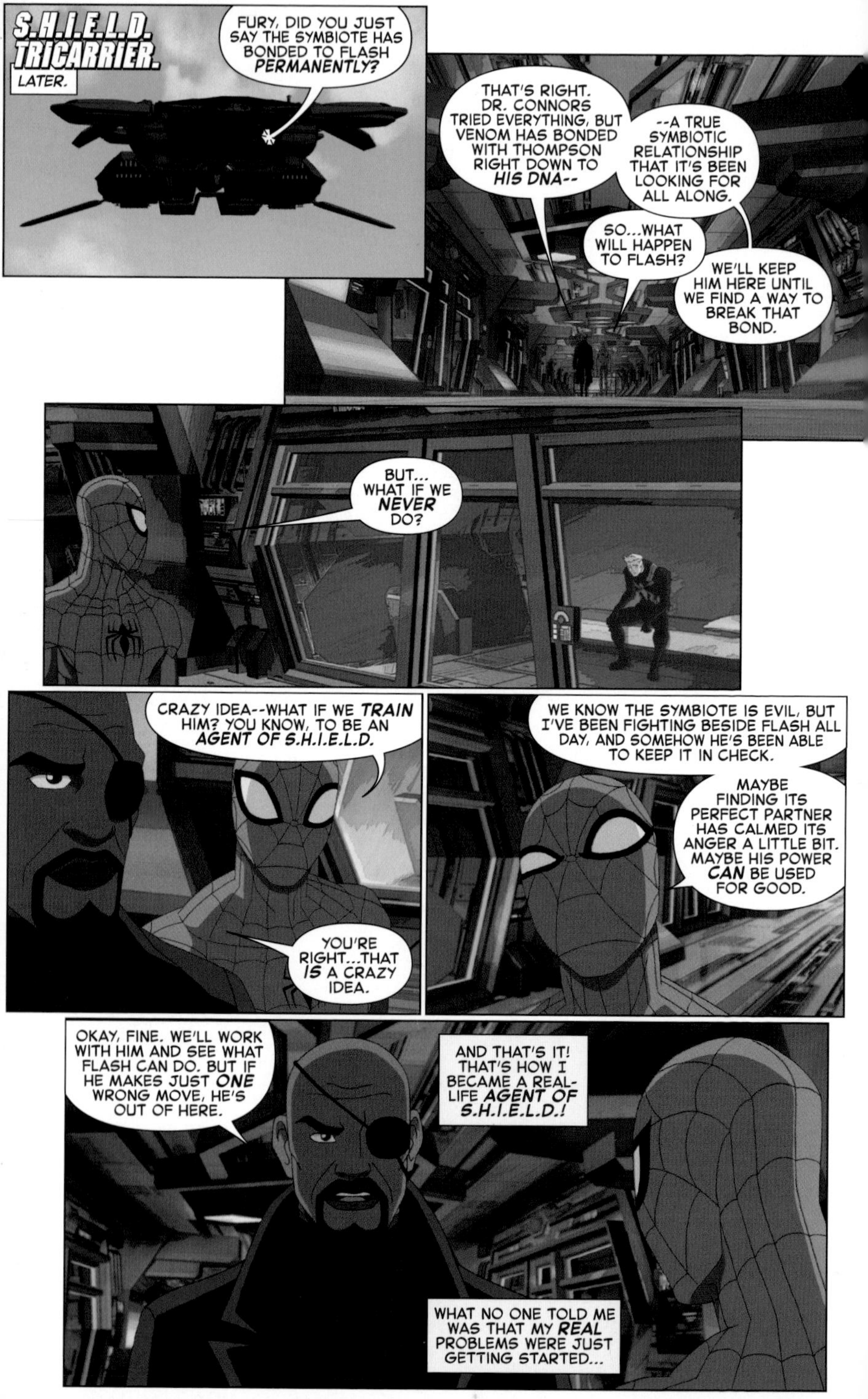
S.H.I.E.L.D. TRICARRIER.
LATER.
FURY, DID YOU JUST SAY THE SYMBIOTE HAS BONDED TO FLASH PERMANENTLY?
THAT'S RIGHT. DR. CONNORS TRIED EVERYTHING, BUT VENOM HAS BONDED WITH THOMPSON RIGHT DOWN TO HIS DNA--
--A TRUE SYMBIOTIC RELATIONSHIP THAT IT'S BEEN LOOKING FOR ALL ALONG.
SO...WHAT WILL HAPPEN TO FLASH?
WE'LL KEEP HIM HERE UNTIL WE FIND A WAY TO BREAK THAT BOND.
BUT... WHAT IF WE NEVER DO?
CRAZY IDEA--WHAT IF WE TRAIN HIM? YOU KNOW, TO BE AN AGENT OF S.H.I.E.L.D.
YOU'RE RIGHT...THAT IS A CRAZY IDEA.
WE KNOW THE SYMBIOTE IS EVIL, BUT I'VE BEEN FIGHTING BESIDE FLASH ALL DAY, AND SOMEHOW HE'S BEEN ABLE TO KEEP IT IN CHECK.
MAYBE FINDING ITS PERFECT PARTNER HAS CALMED ITS ANGER A LITTLE BIT. MAYBE HIS POWER CAN BE USED FOR GOOD.
OKAY, FINE. WE'LL WORK WITH FLASH AND SEE WHAT FLASH CAN DO. BUT IF HE MAKES JUST ONE WRONG MOVE, HE'S OUT OF HERE.
AND THAT'S IT! THAT'S HOW I BECAME A REAL-LIFE AGENT OF S.H.I.E.L.D.!
WHAT NO ONE TOLD ME WAS THAT MY REAL PROBLEMS WERE JUST GETTING STARTED...

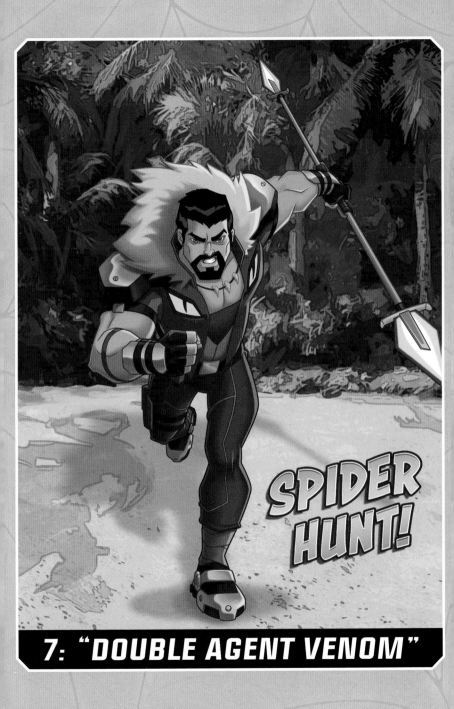

SPIDER HUNT!

7: "DOUBLE AGENT VENOM"

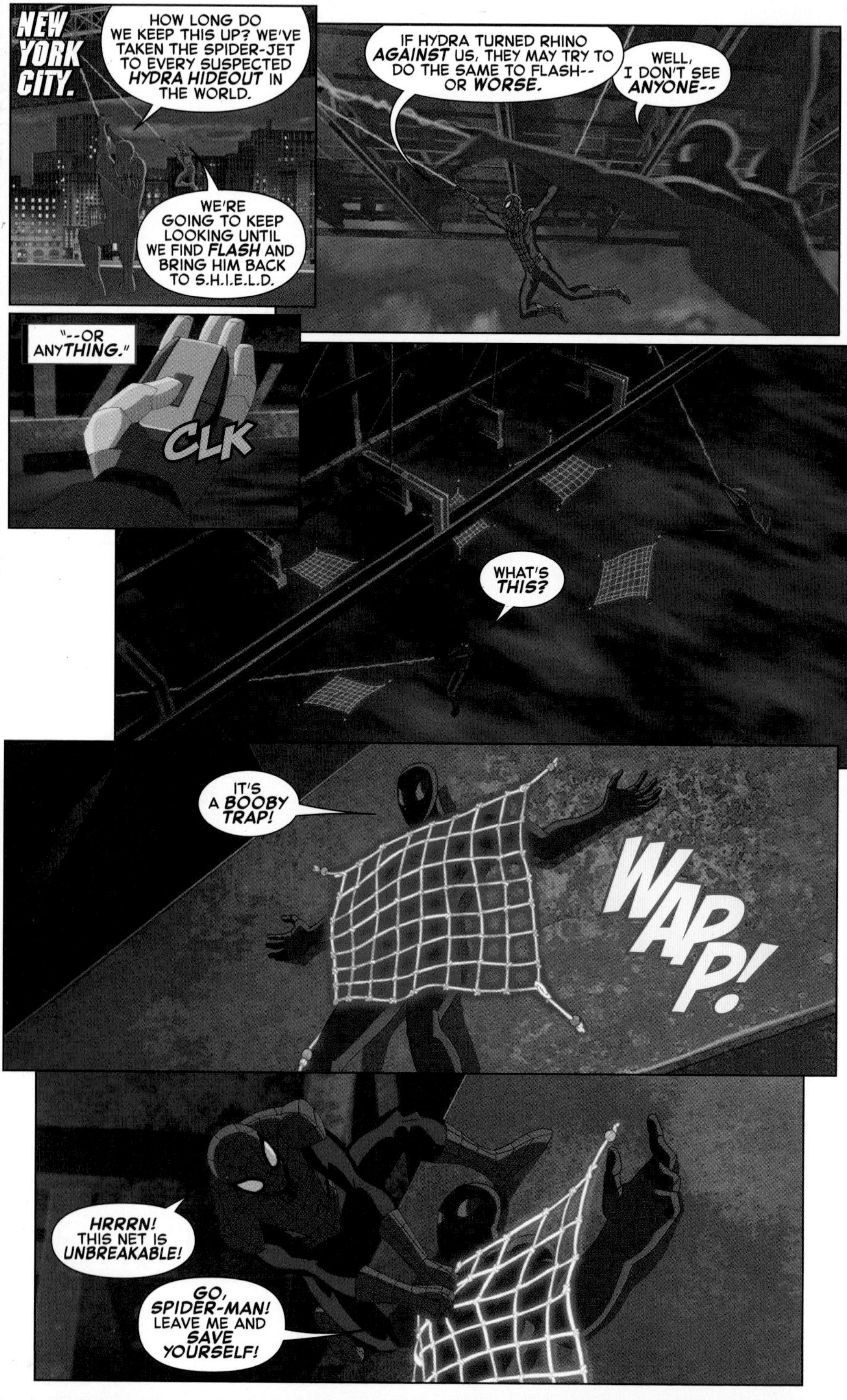
NEW YORK CITY.
HOW LONG DO WE KEEP THIS UP? WE'VE TAKEN THE SPIDER-JET TO EVERY SUSPECTED HYDRA HIDEOUT IN THE WORLD.
WE'RE GOING TO KEEP LOOKING UNTIL WE FIND FLASH AND BRING HIM BACK TO S.H.I.E.L.D.
IF HYDRA TURNED RHINO AGAINST US, THEY MAY TRY TO DO THE SAME TO FLASH-- OR WORSE.
WELL, I DON'T SEE ANYONE--
"--OR ANYTHING."
CLK
WHAT'S THIS?
IT'S A BOOBY TRAP!
WAP!
HRRRN! THIS NET IS UNBREAKABLE!
GO, SPIDER-MAN! LEAVE ME AND SAVE YOURSELF!

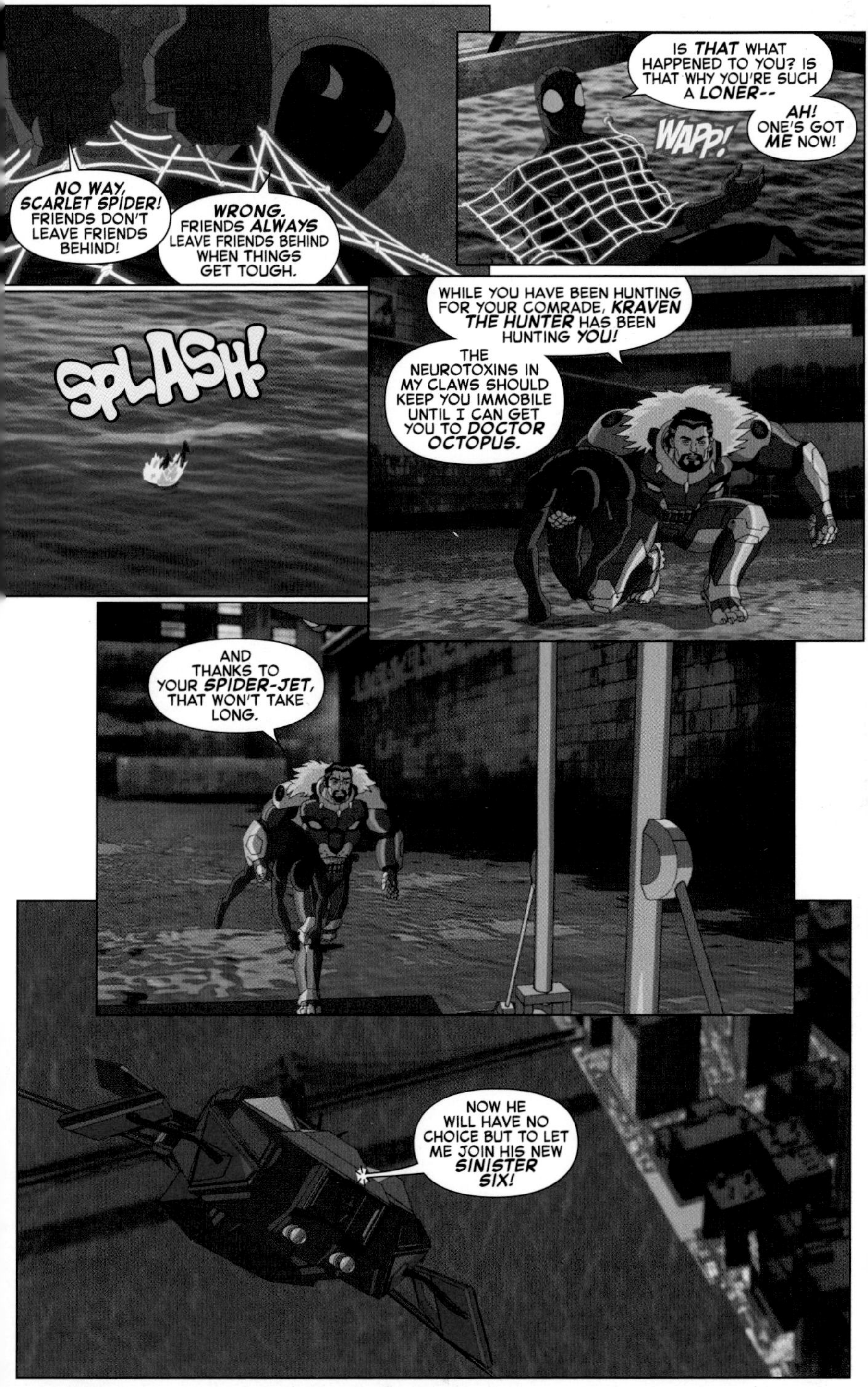
NO WAY, SCARLET SPIDER! FRIENDS DON'T LEAVE FRIENDS BEHIND!
WRONG. FRIENDS ALWAYS LEAVE FRIENDS BEHIND WHEN THINGS GET TOUGH.
IS THAT WHAT HAPPENED TO YOU? IS THAT WHY YOU'RE SUCH A LONER--
WAPP!
AH! ONE'S GOT ME NOW!
SPLASH!
WHILE YOU HAVE BEEN HUNTING FOR YOUR COMRADE, KRAVEN THE HUNTER HAS BEEN HUNTING YOU!
THE NEUROTOXINS IN MY CLAWS SHOULD KEEP YOU IMMOBILE UNTIL I CAN GET YOU TO DOCTOR OCTOPUS.
AND THANKS TO YOUR SPIDER-JET, THAT WON'T TAKE LONG.
NOW HE WILL HAVE NO CHOICE BUT TO LET ME JOIN HIS NEW SINISTER SIX!

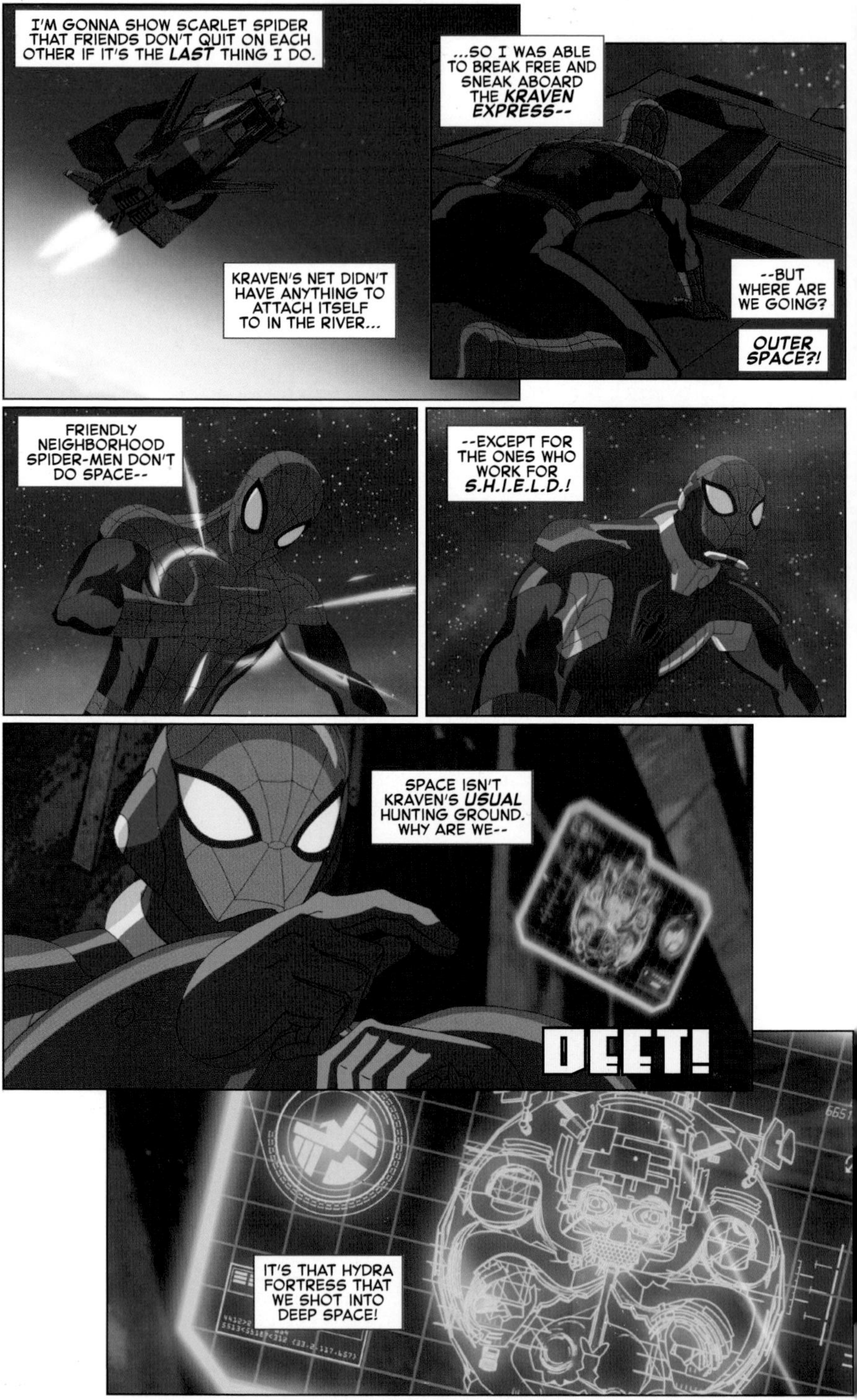
I'M GONNA SHOW SCARLET SPIDER THAT FRIENDS DON'T QUIT ON EACH OTHER IF IT'S THE LAST THING I DO.
KRAVEN'S NET DIDN'T HAVE ANYTHING TO ATTACH ITSELF TO IN THE RIVER...
...SO I WAS ABLE TO BREAK FREE AND SNEAK ABOARD THE KRAVEN EXPRESS--
--BUT WHERE ARE WE GOING?
OUTER SPACE?!
FRIENDLY NEIGHBORHOOD SPIDER-MEN DON'T DO SPACE--
--EXCEPT FOR THE ONES WHO WORK FOR S.H.I.E.L.D.!
SPACE ISN'T KRAVEN'S USUAL HUNTING GROUND. WHY ARE WE--
DEET!
IT'S THAT HYDRA FORTRESS THAT WE SHOT INTO DEEP SPACE!

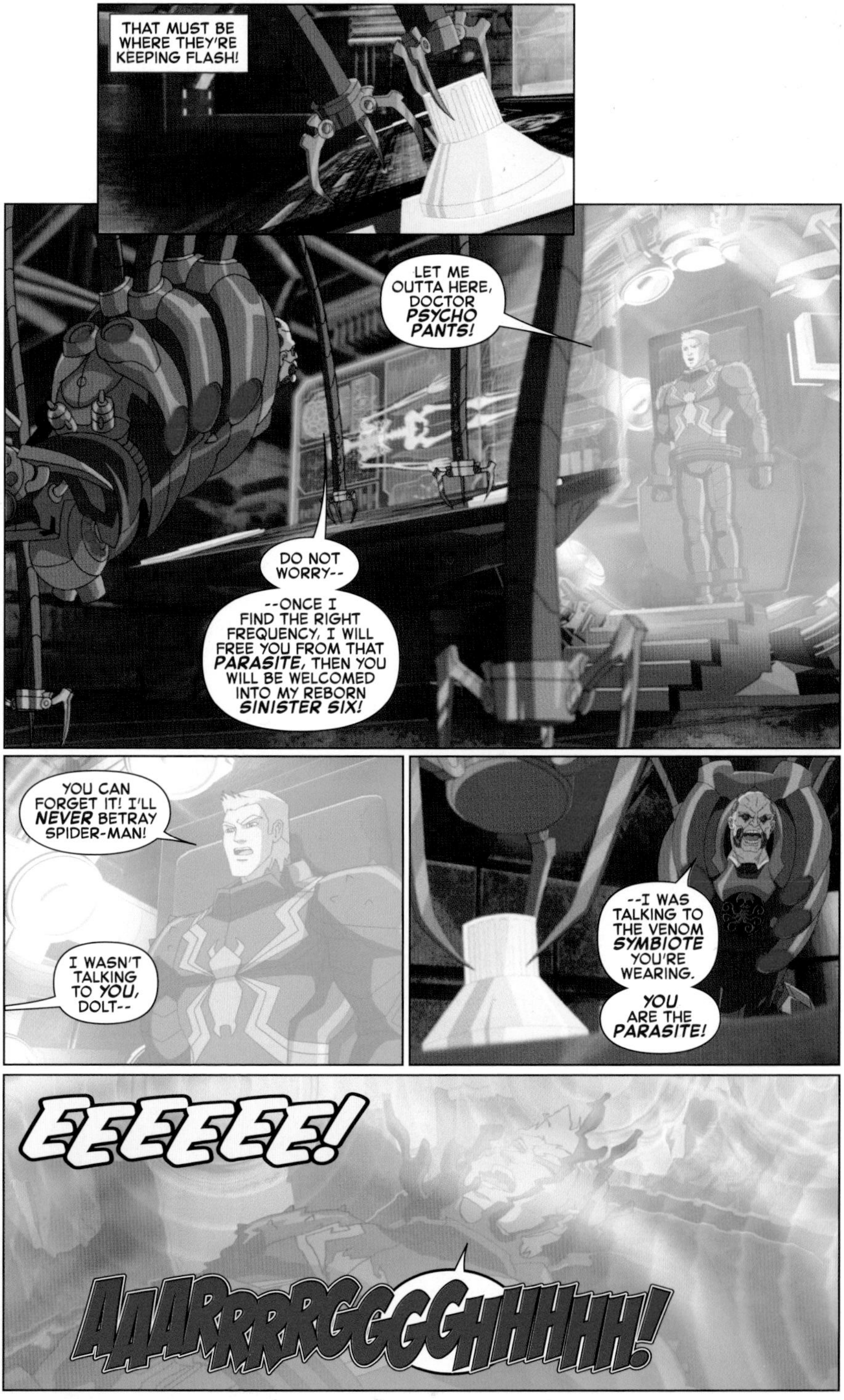
THAT MUST BE WHERE THEY'RE KEEPING FLASH!
LET ME OUTTA HERE, DOCTOR PSYCHO PANTS!
DO NOT WORRY--
--ONCE I FIND THE RIGHT FREQUENCY, I WILL FREE YOU FROM THAT PARASITE, THEN YOU WILL BE WELCOMED INTO MY REBORN SINISTER SIX!
YOU CAN FORGET IT! I'LL NEVER BETRAY SPIDER-MAN!
I WASN'T TALKING TO YOU, DOLT--
--I WAS TALKING TO THE VENOM SYMBIOTE YOU'RE WEARING.
YOU ARE THE PARASITE!
EEEEEE!
AAARRRRGGGGHHHHH!

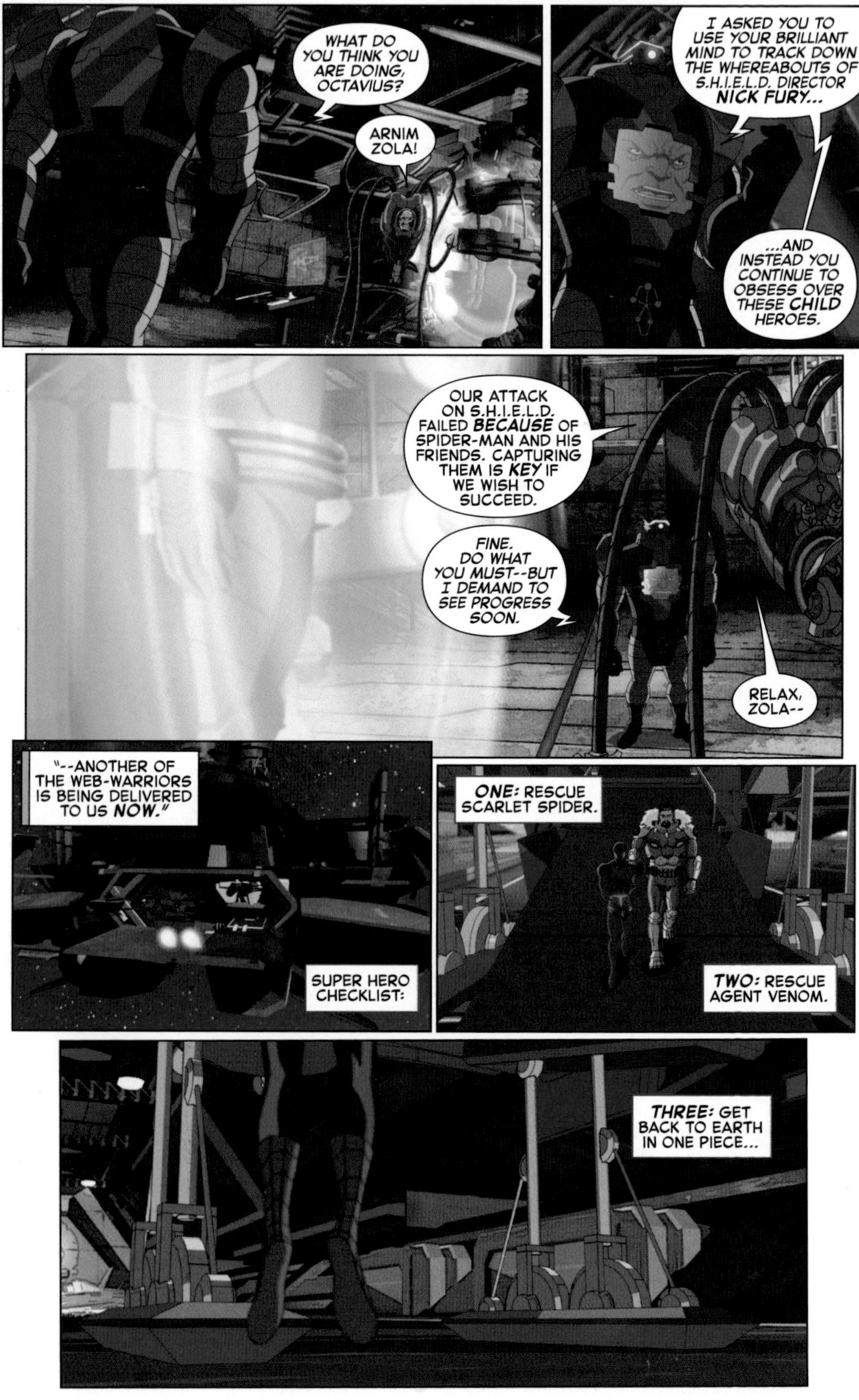
WHAT DO YOU THINK YOU ARE DOING, OCTAVIUS?
ARNIM ZOLA!
I ASKED YOU TO USE YOUR BRILLIANT MIND TO TRACK DOWN THE WHEREABOUTS OF S.H.I.E.L.D. DIRECTOR NICK FURY...
...AND INSTEAD YOU CONTINUE TO OBSESS OVER THESE CHILD HEROES.
OUR ATTACK ON S.H.I.E.L.D. FAILED BECAUSE OF SPIDER-MAN AND HIS FRIENDS. CAPTURING THEM IS KEY IF WE WISH TO SUCCEED.
FINE. DO WHAT YOU MUST--BUT I DEMAND TO SEE PROGRESS SOON.
RELAX, ZOLA--
"--ANOTHER OF THE WEB-WARRIORS IS BEING DELIVERED TO US NOW."
SUPER HERO CHECKLIST:
ONE: RESCUE SCARLET SPIDER.
TWO: RESCUE AGENT VENOM.
THREE: GET BACK TO EARTH IN ONE PIECE...

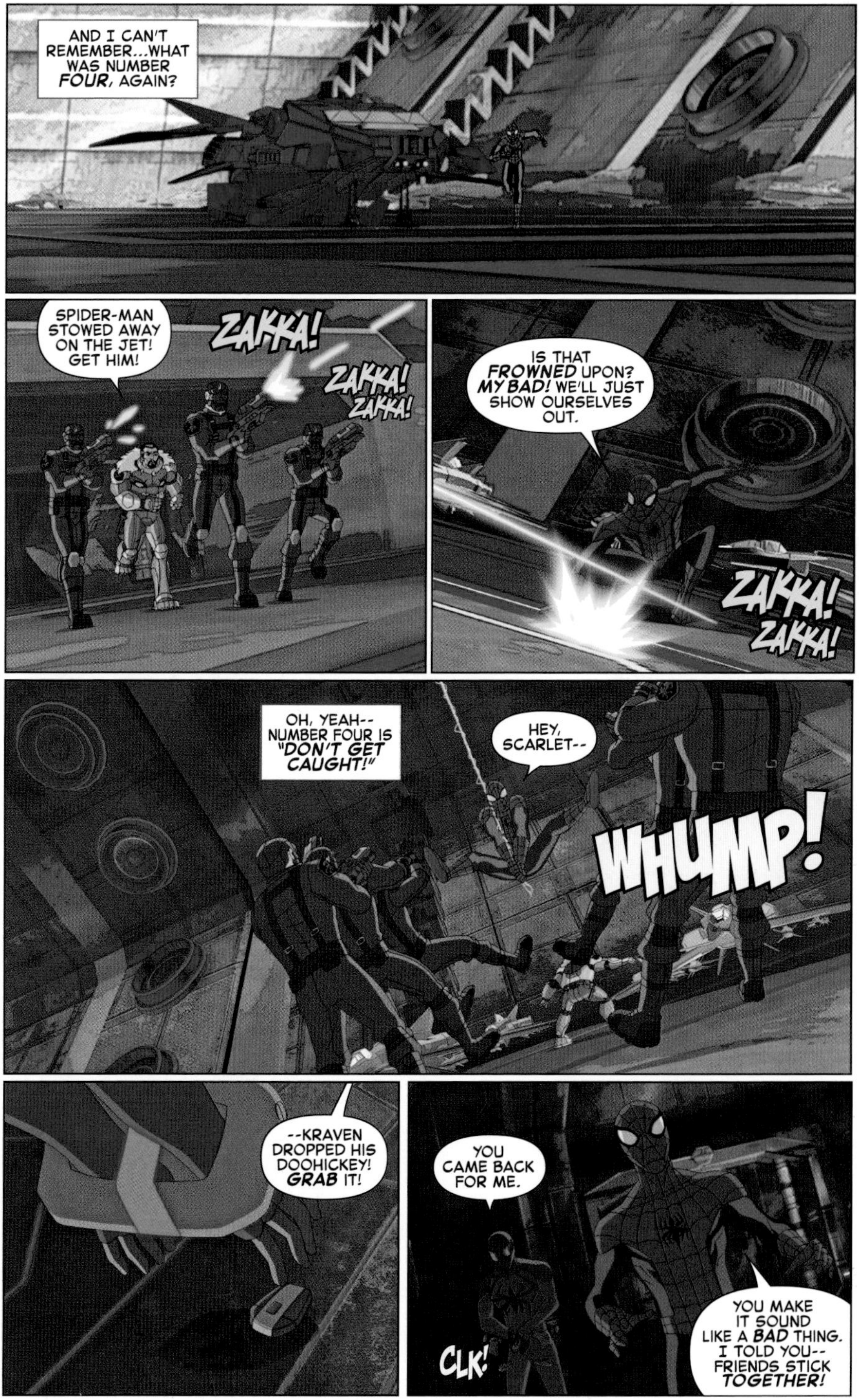
AND I CAN'T REMEMBER...WHAT WAS NUMBER FOUR, AGAIN?
SPIDER-MAN STOWED AWAY ON THE JET! GET HIM!
ZAKKA!
ZAKKA! ZAKKA!
IS THAT FROWNED UPON? MY BAD! WE'LL JUST SHOW OURSELVES OUT.
ZAKKA! ZAKKA!
OH, YEAH-- NUMBER FOUR IS "DON'T GET CAUGHT!"
HEY, SCARLET--
WHUMP!
--KRAVEN DROPPED HIS DOOHICKEY! GRAB IT!
YOU CAME BACK FOR ME.
CLK!
YOU MAKE IT SOUND LIKE A BAD THING. I TOLD YOU-- FRIENDS STICK TOGETHER!

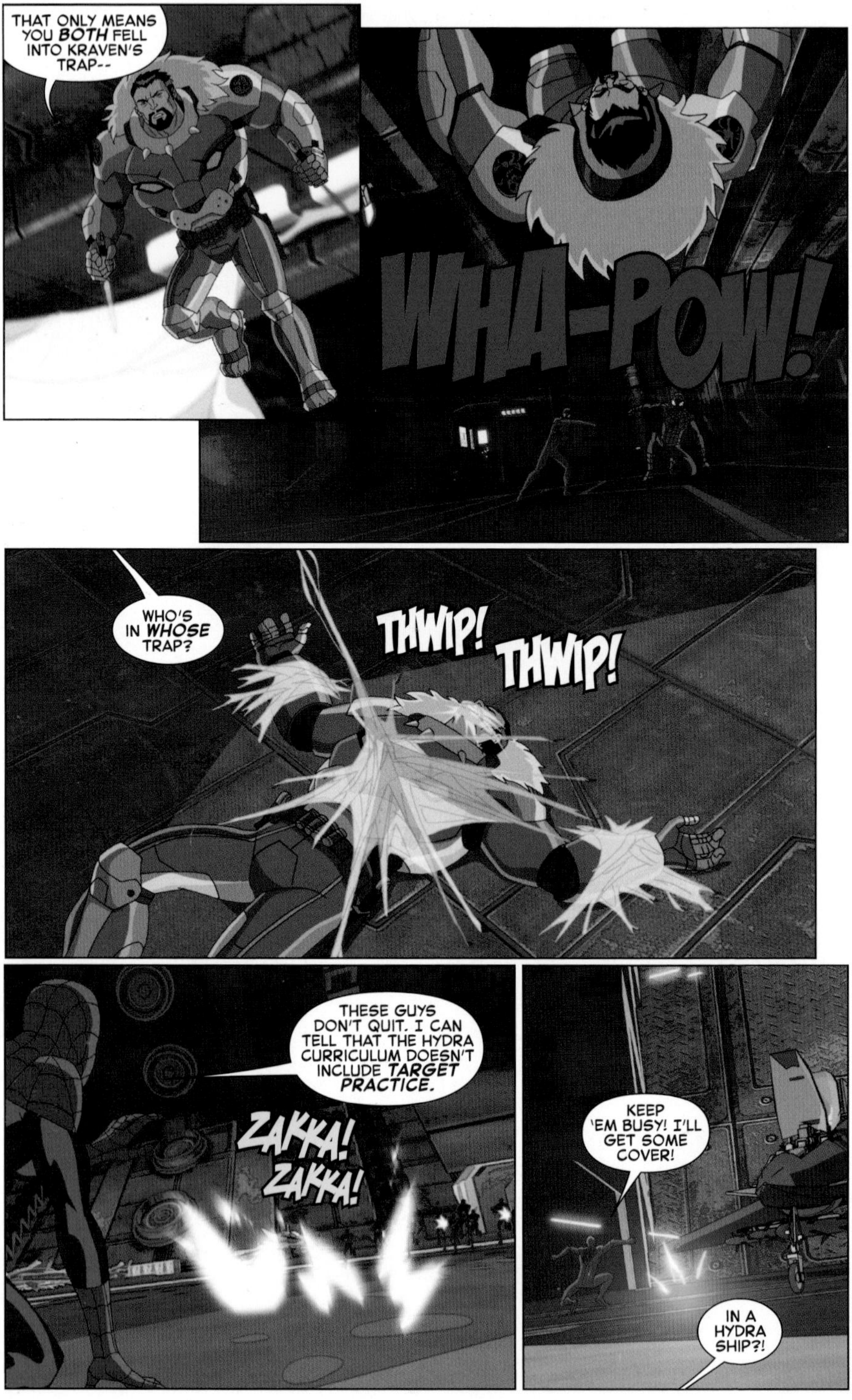
THAT ONLY MEANS YOU BOTH FELL INTO KRAVEN'S TRAP--
WHA-POW!
WHO'S IN WHOSE TRAP?
THWIP! THWIP!
THESE GUYS DON'T QUIT. I CAN TELL THAT THE HYDRA CURRICULUM DOESN'T INCLUDE TARGET PRACTICE.
ZAKKA! ZAKKA!
KEEP 'EM BUSY! I'LL GET SOME COVER!
IN A HYDRA SHIP?!

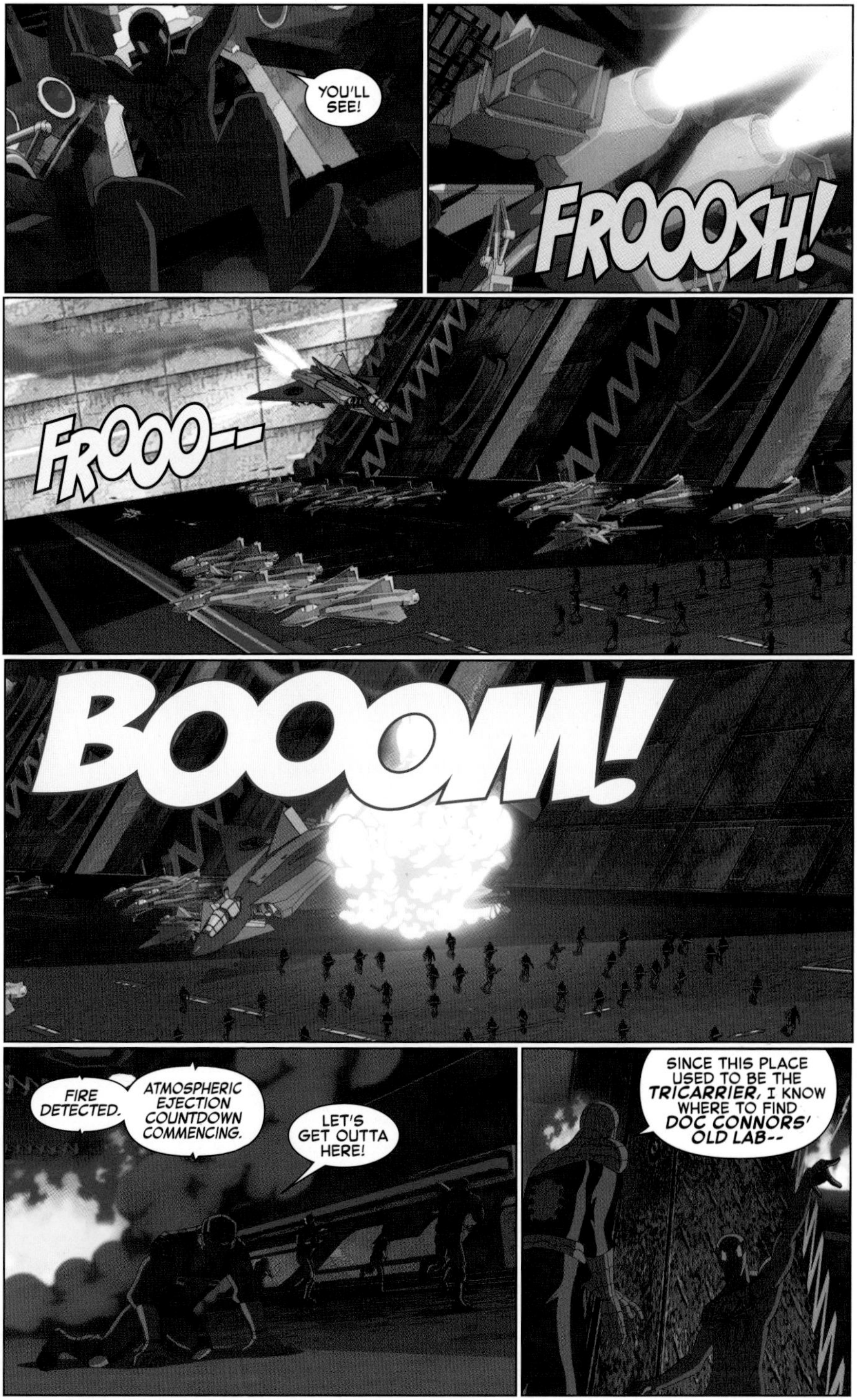
YOU'LL SEE!
FROOOSH!
FROOO--
BOOOM!
FIRE DETECTED.
ATMOSPHERIC EJECTION COUNTDOWN COMMENCING.
LET'S GET OUTTA HERE!
SINCE THIS PLACE USED TO BE THE *TRICARRIER*, I KNOW WHERE TO FIND *DOC CONNORS'* OLD LAB--

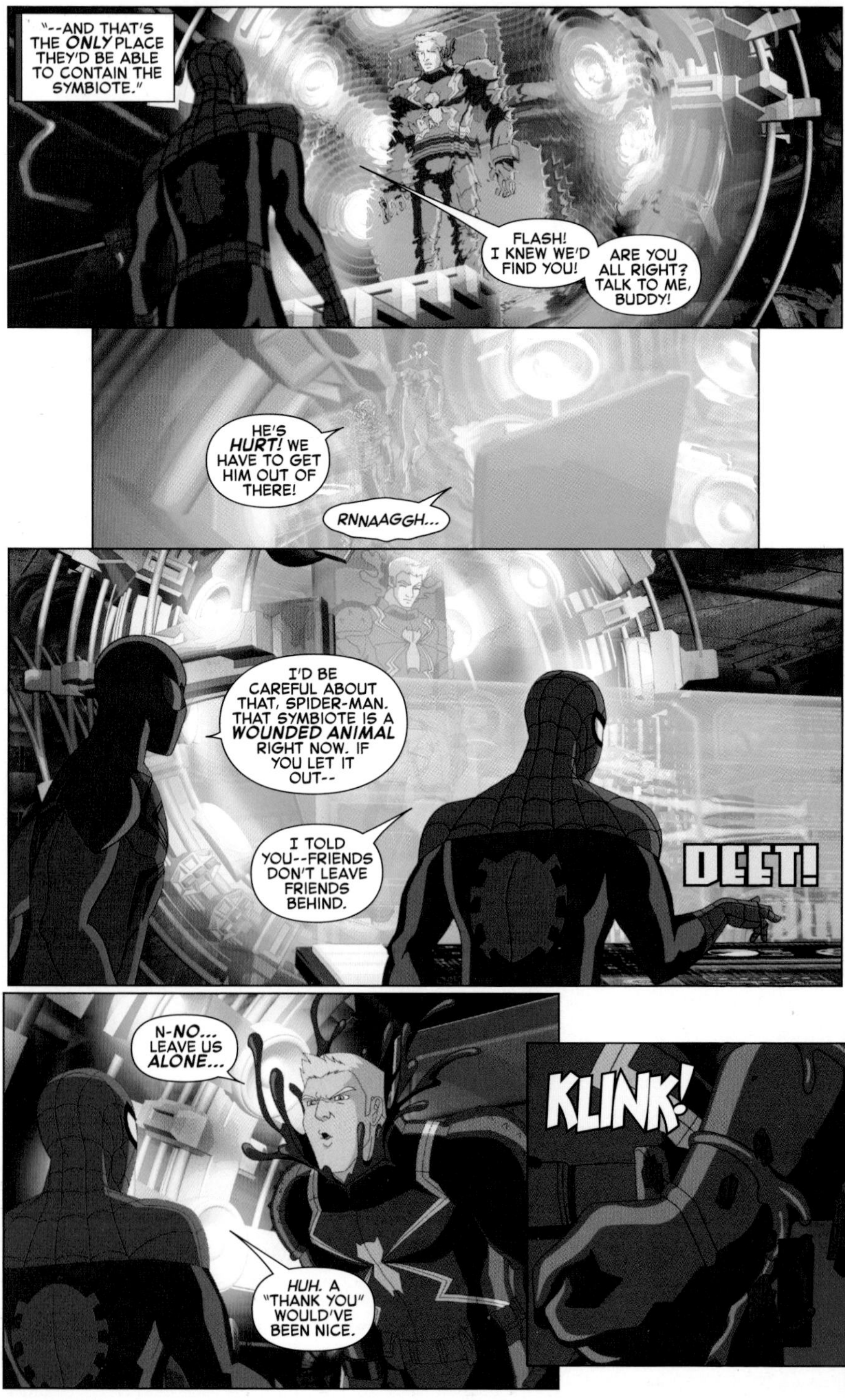
"--AND THAT'S THE ONLY PLACE THEY'D BE ABLE TO CONTAIN THE SYMBIOTE."
FLASH! I KNEW WE'D FIND YOU!
ARE YOU ALL RIGHT? TALK TO ME, BUDDY!
HE'S HURT! WE HAVE TO GET HIM OUT OF THERE!
RNNAAGGH...
I'D BE CAREFUL ABOUT THAT, SPIDER-MAN. THAT SYMBIOTE IS A WOUNDED ANIMAL RIGHT NOW. IF YOU LET IT OUT--
I TOLD YOU--FRIENDS DON'T LEAVE FRIENDS BEHIND.
DEET!
N-NO... LEAVE US ALONE...
HUH. A "THANK YOU" WOULD'VE BEEN NICE.
KLINK!

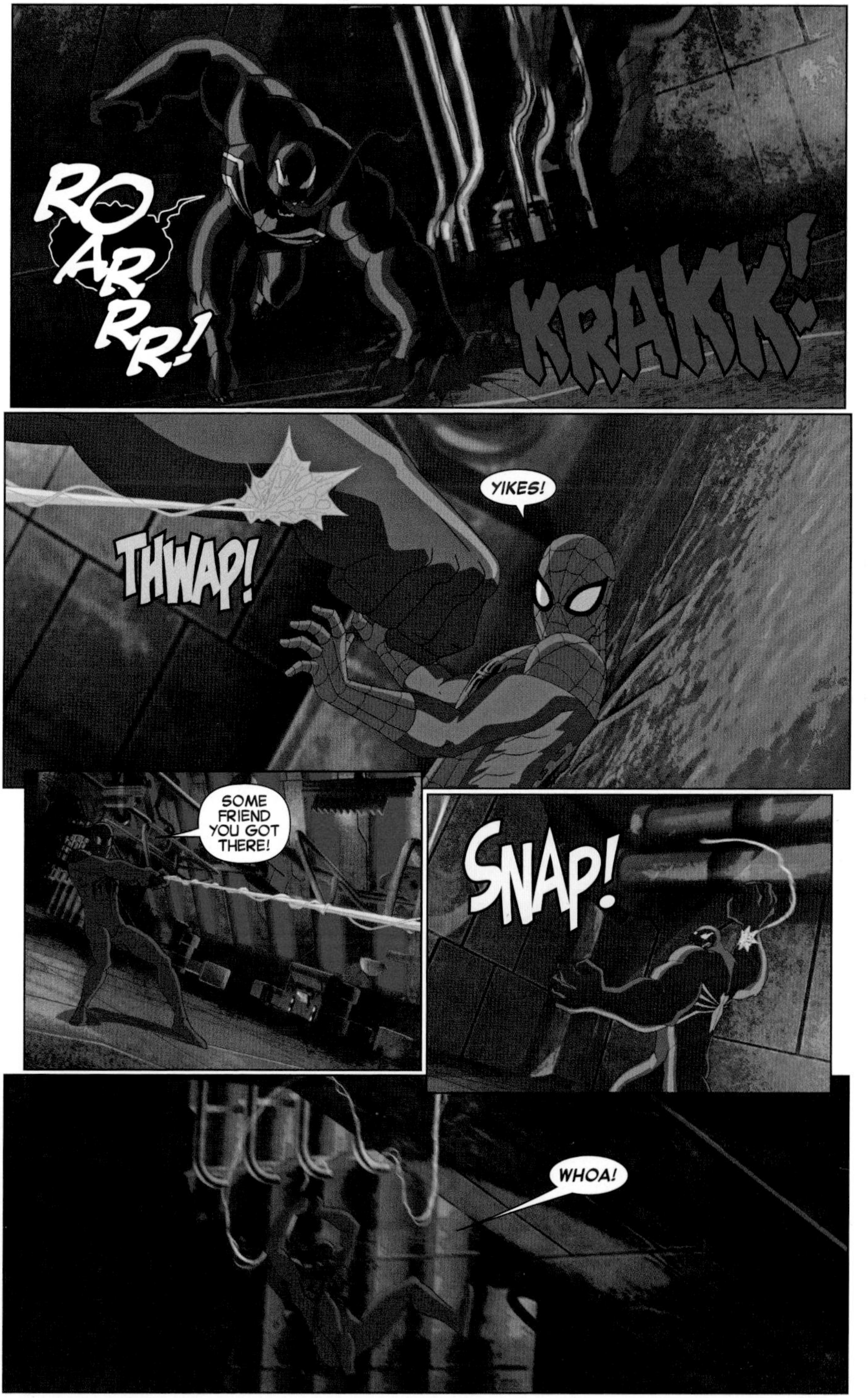
ROARRR!
KRAKK!
THWAP!
YIKES!
SOME FRIEND YOU GOT THERE!
SNAP!
WHOA!

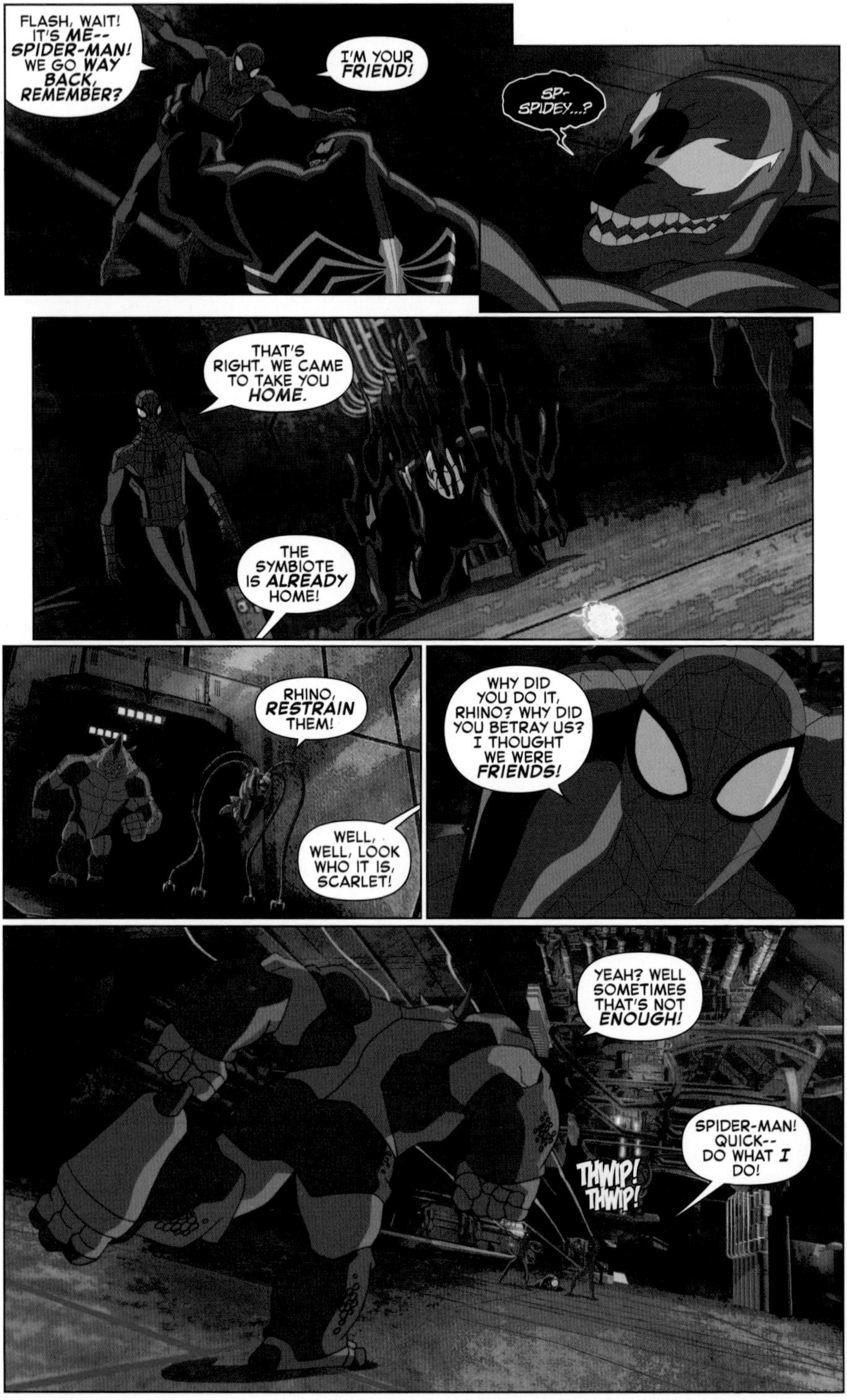
FLASH, WAIT! IT'S ME--SPIDER-MAN! WE GO WAY BACK, REMEMBER?
I'M YOUR FRIEND!
SP-SPIDEY...?
THAT'S RIGHT. WE CAME TO TAKE YOU HOME.
THE SYMBIOTE IS ALREADY HOME!
RHINO, RESTRAIN THEM!
WELL, WELL, LOOK WHO IT IS, SCARLET!
WHY DID YOU DO IT, RHINO? WHY DID YOU BETRAY US? I THOUGHT WE WERE FRIENDS!
YEAH? WELL SOMETIMES THAT'S NOT ENOUGH!
SPIDER-MAN! QUICK--DO WHAT I DO!
THWIP! THWIP!

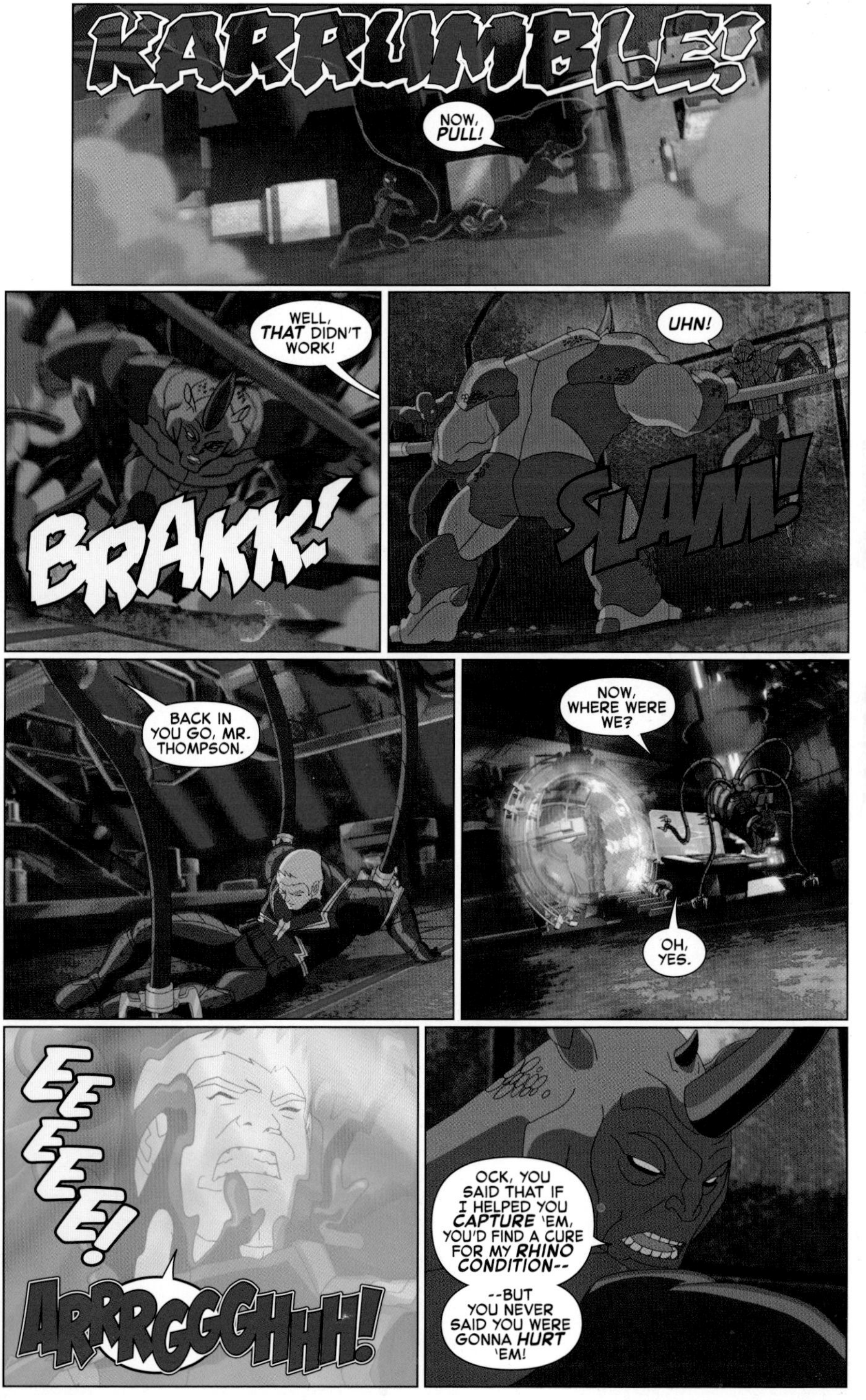
KARRUMBLE!
NOW, PULL!
WELL, THAT DIDN'T WORK!
BRAKK!
UHN!
SLAM!
BACK IN YOU GO, MR. THOMPSON.
NOW, WHERE WERE WE?
OH, YES.
EEEEEE!
ARRRGGGHHH!
OCK, YOU SAID THAT IF I HELPED YOU CAPTURE 'EM, YOU'D FIND A CURE FOR MY RHINO CONDITION--
--BUT YOU NEVER SAID YOU WERE GONNA HURT 'EM!

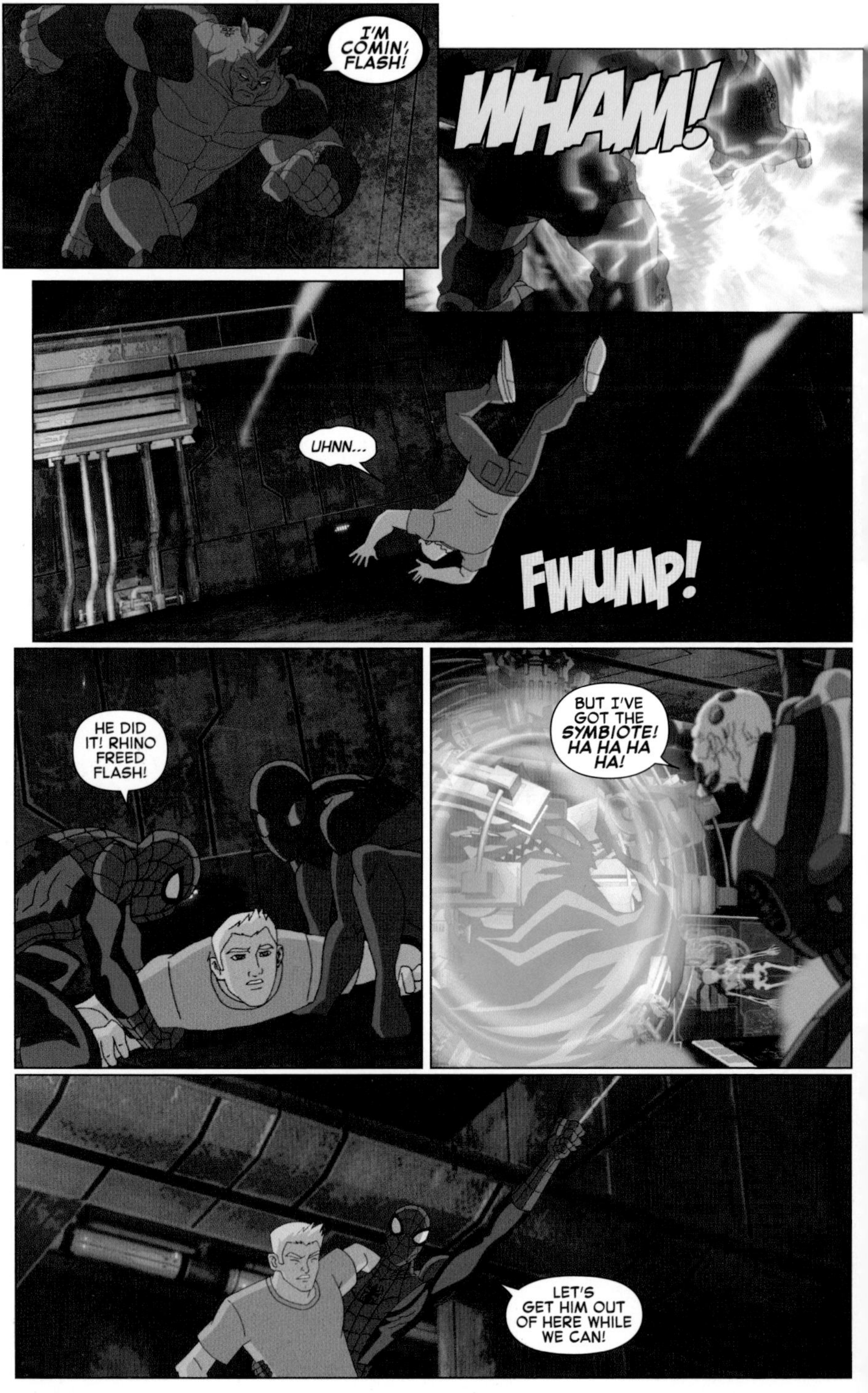
I'M COMIN', FLASH!
WHAM!
UHNN...
FWUMP!
HE DID IT! RHINO FREED FLASH!
BUT I'VE GOT THE SYMBIOTE! HA HA HA HA!
LET'S GET HIM OUT OF HERE WHILE WE CAN!

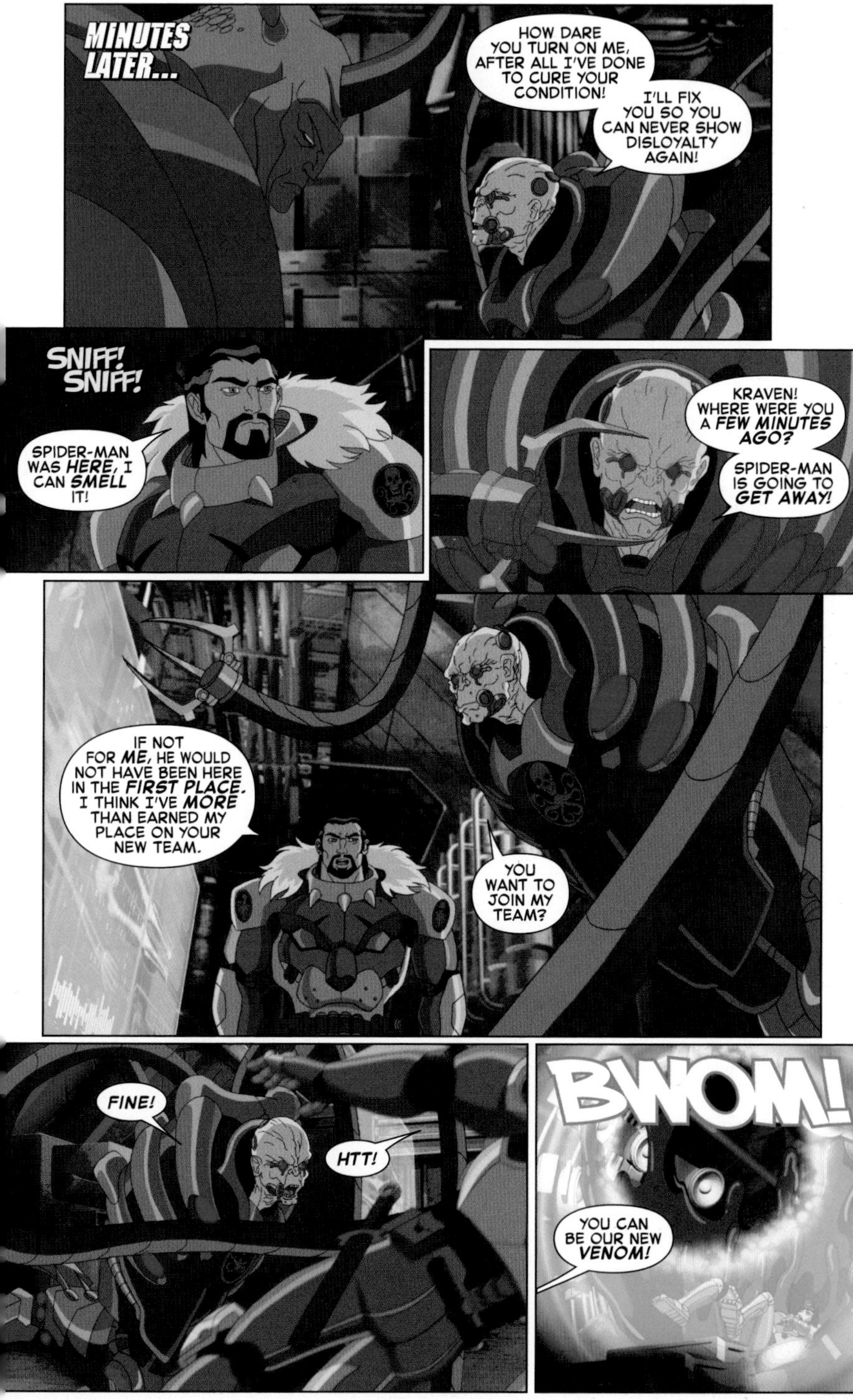
MINUTES LATER...
HOW DARE YOU TURN ON ME, AFTER ALL I'VE DONE TO CURE YOUR CONDITION!
I'LL FIX YOU SO YOU CAN NEVER SHOW DISLOYALTY AGAIN!
SNIFF! SNIFF!
SPIDER-MAN WAS HERE, I CAN SMELL IT!
KRAVEN! WHERE WERE YOU A FEW MINUTES AGO?
SPIDER-MAN IS GOING TO GET AWAY!
IF NOT FOR ME, HE WOULD NOT HAVE BEEN HERE IN THE FIRST PLACE. I THINK I'VE MORE THAN EARNED MY PLACE ON YOUR NEW TEAM.
YOU WANT TO JOIN MY TEAM?
FINE!
HTT!
BWOM!
YOU CAN BE OUR NEW VENOM!

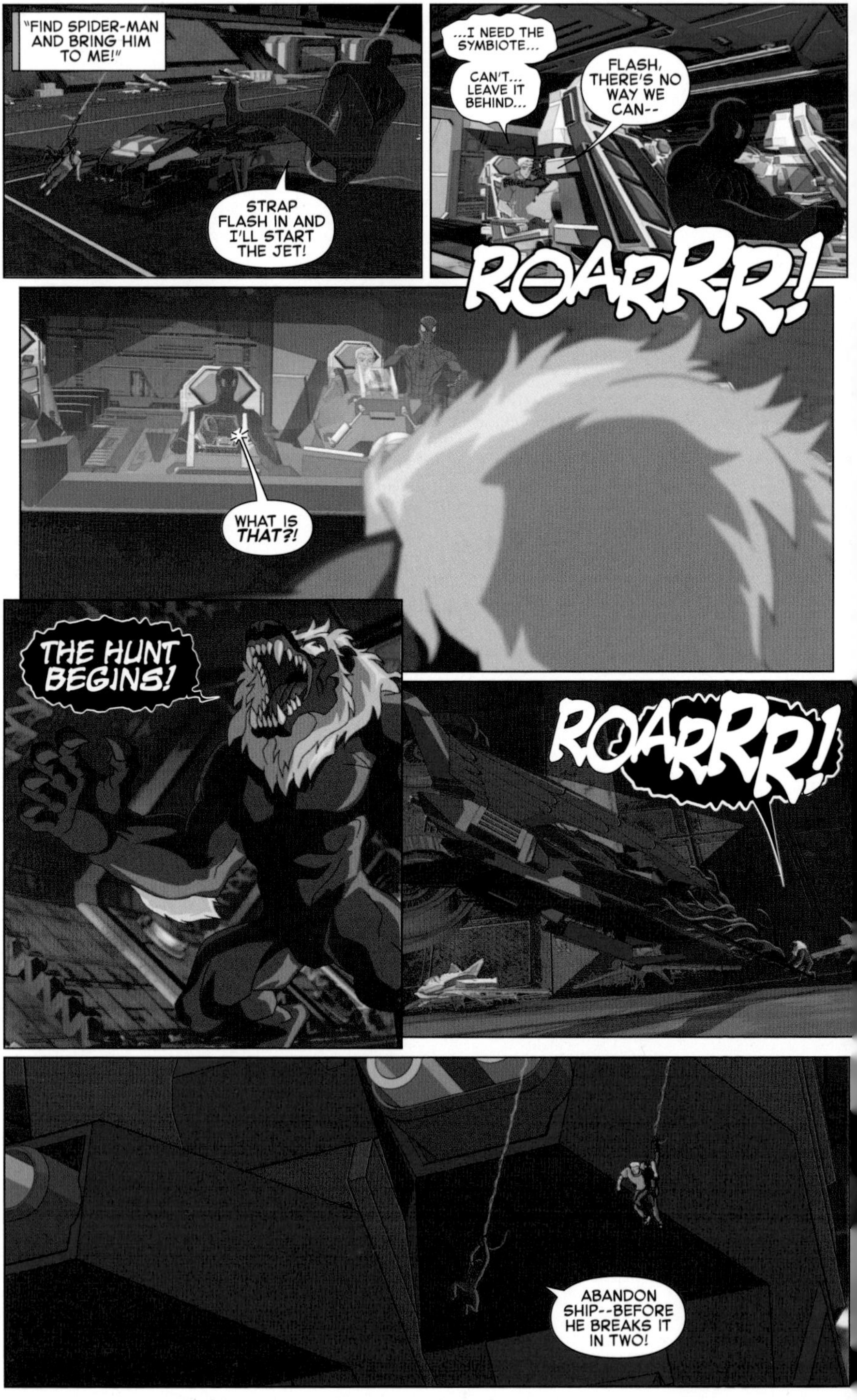
"FIND SPIDER-MAN AND BRING HIM TO ME!"
STRAP FLASH IN AND I'LL START THE JET!
...I NEED THE SYMBIOTE...
CAN'T... LEAVE IT BEHIND...
FLASH, THERE'S NO WAY WE CAN--
ROARRR!
WHAT IS THAT?!
THE HUNT BEGINS!
ROARRR!
ABANDON SHIP--BEFORE HE BREAKS IT IN TWO!

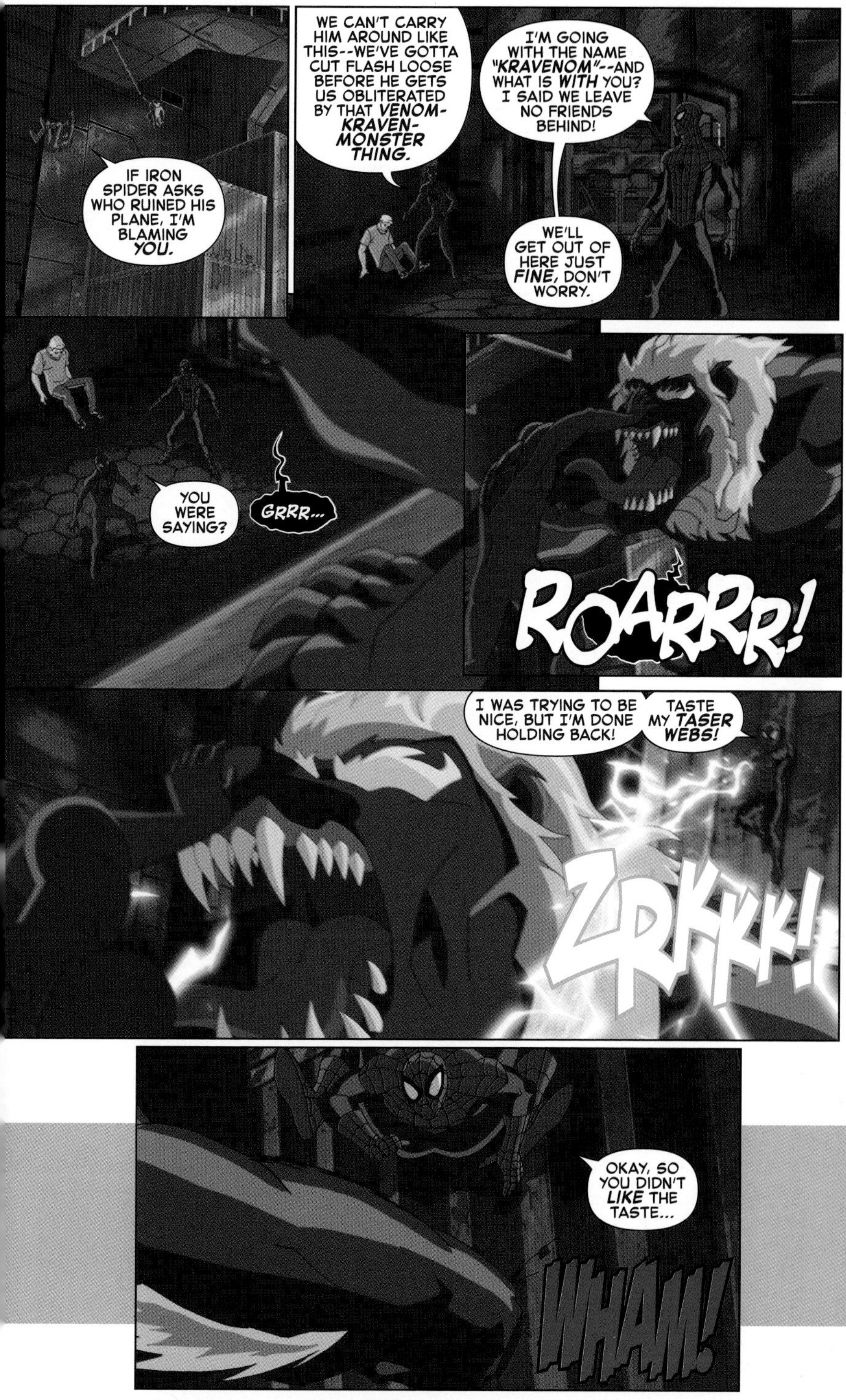

IF IRON SPIDER ASKS WHO RUINED HIS PLANE, I'M BLAMING YOU.
WE CAN'T CARRY HIM AROUND LIKE THIS--WE'VE GOTTA CUT FLASH LOOSE BEFORE HE GETS US OBLITERATED BY THAT VENOM-KRAVEN-MONSTER THING.
I'M GOING WITH THE NAME "KRAVENOM"--AND WHAT IS WITH YOU? I SAID WE LEAVE NO FRIENDS BEHIND!
WE'LL GET OUT OF HERE JUST FINE, DON'T WORRY.
YOU WERE SAYING?
GRRR...
ROARRR!
I WAS TRYING TO BE NICE, BUT I'M DONE HOLDING BACK!
TASTE MY TASER WEBS!
ZRKKK!
OKAY, SO YOU DIDN'T LIKE THE TASTE...
WHAM!

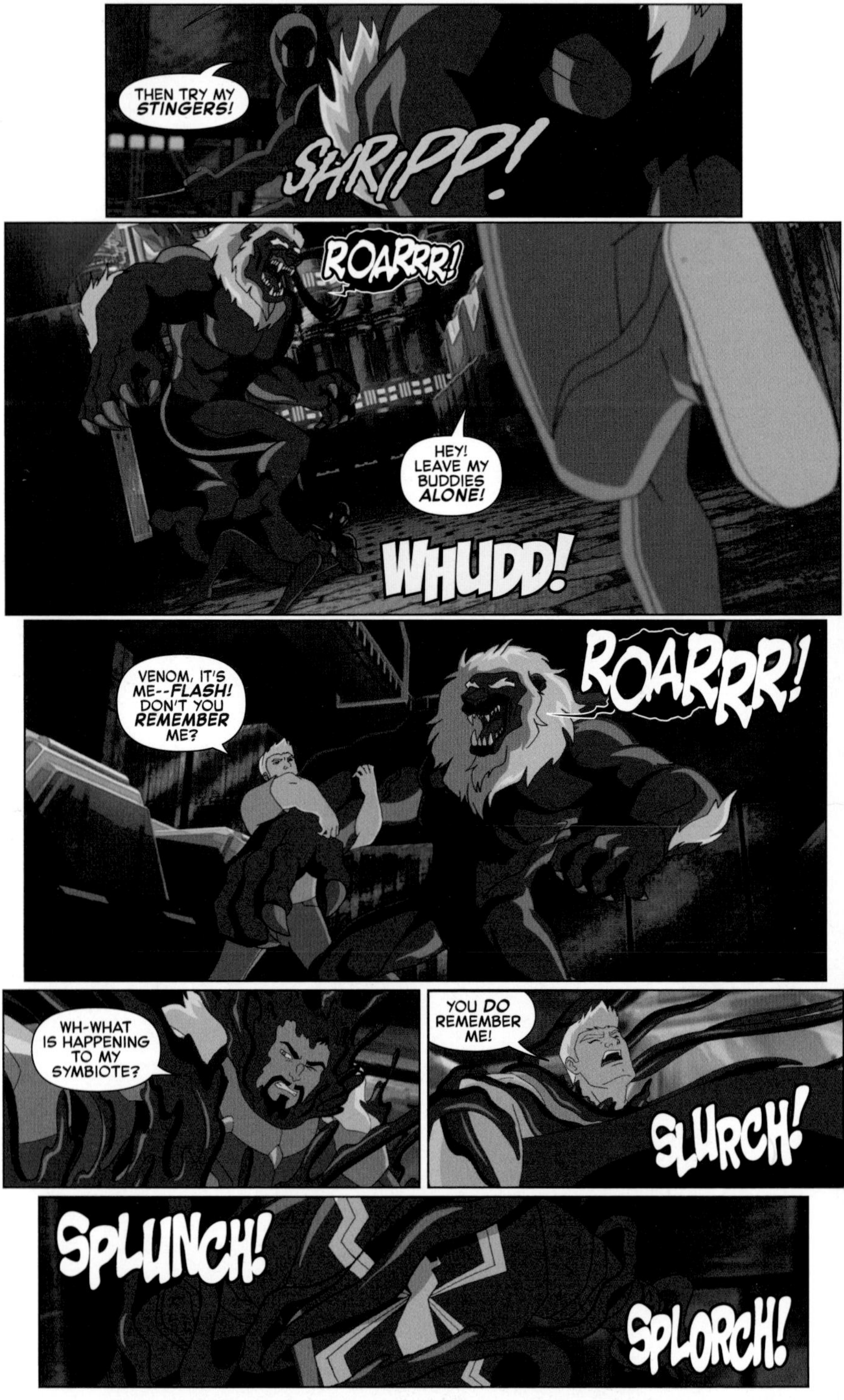
THEN TRY MY STINGERS!
SHRIPP!
ROARRR!
HEY! LEAVE MY BUDDIES ALONE!
WHUDD!
VENOM, IT'S ME--FLASH! DON'T YOU REMEMBER ME?
ROARRR!
WH-WHAT IS HAPPENING TO MY SYMBIOTE?
YOU DO REMEMBER ME!
SLURCH!
SPLUNCH!
SPLORCH!

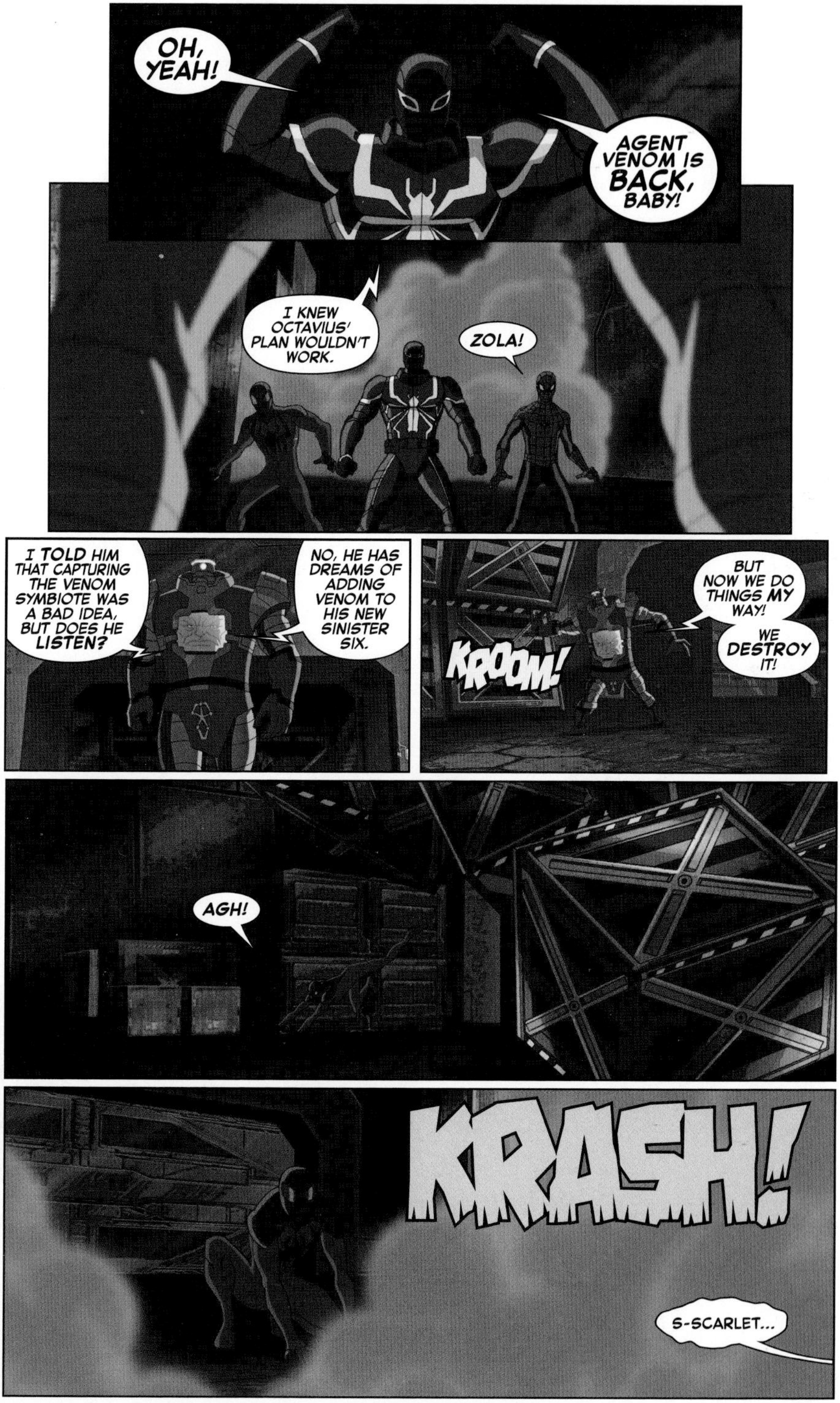
OH, YEAH!
AGENT VENOM IS BACK, BABY!
I KNEW OCTAVIUS' PLAN WOULDN'T WORK.
ZOLA!
I TOLD HIM THAT CAPTURING THE VENOM SYMBIOTE WAS A BAD IDEA, BUT DOES HE LISTEN?
NO, HE HAS DREAMS OF ADDING VENOM TO HIS NEW SINISTER SIX.
KROOM!
BUT NOW WE DO THINGS MY WAY!
WE DESTROY IT!
AGH!
KRASH!
S-SCARLET...

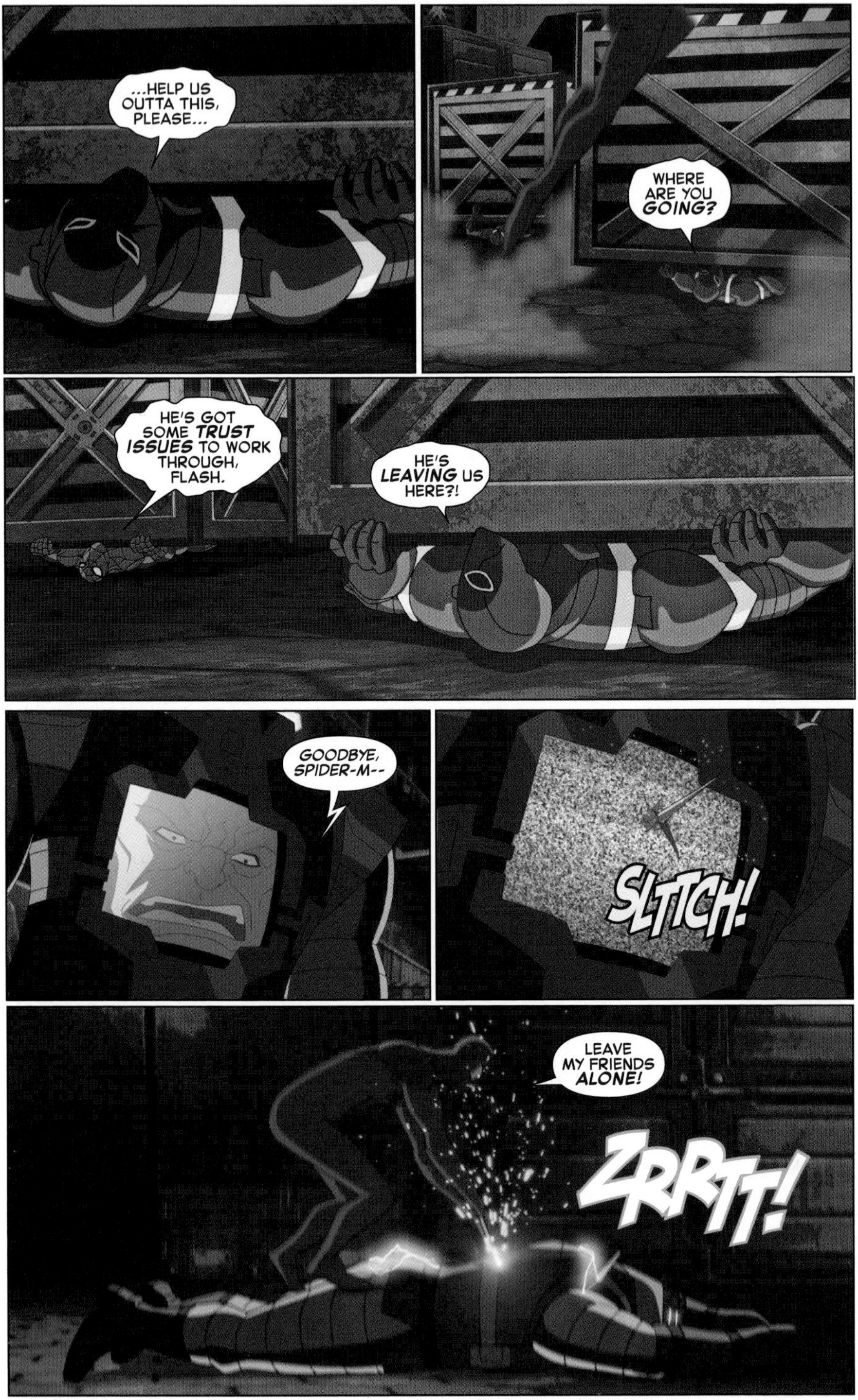
...HELP US OUTTA THIS, PLEASE...
WHERE ARE YOU GOING?
HE'S GOT SOME TRUST ISSUES TO WORK THROUGH, FLASH.
HE'S LEAVING US HERE?!
GOODBYE, SPIDER-M--
SLTTCH!
LEAVE MY FRIENDS ALONE!
ZRRTT!

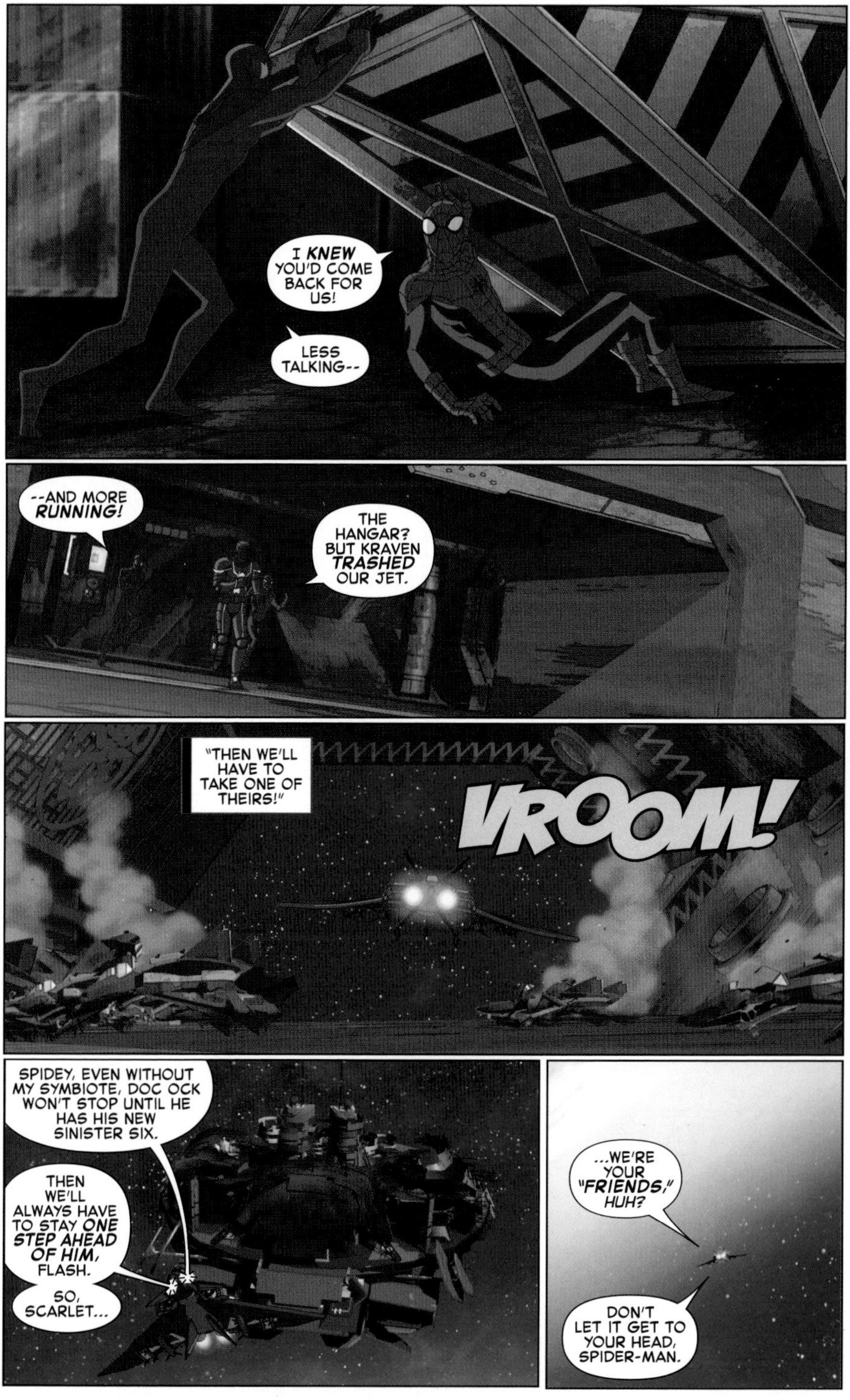
I KNEW YOU'D COME BACK FOR US!
LESS TALKING--
--AND MORE RUNNING!
THE HANGAR? BUT KRAVEN TRASHED OUR JET.
"THEN WE'LL HAVE TO TAKE ONE OF THEIRS!"
VROOM!
SPIDEY, EVEN WITHOUT MY SYMBIOTE, DOC OCK WON'T STOP UNTIL HE HAS HIS NEW SINISTER SIX.
THEN WE'LL ALWAYS HAVE TO STAY ONE STEP AHEAD OF HIM, FLASH.
SO, SCARLET...
...WE'RE YOUR "FRIENDS," HUH?
DON'T LET IT GET TO YOUR HEAD, SPIDER-MAN.

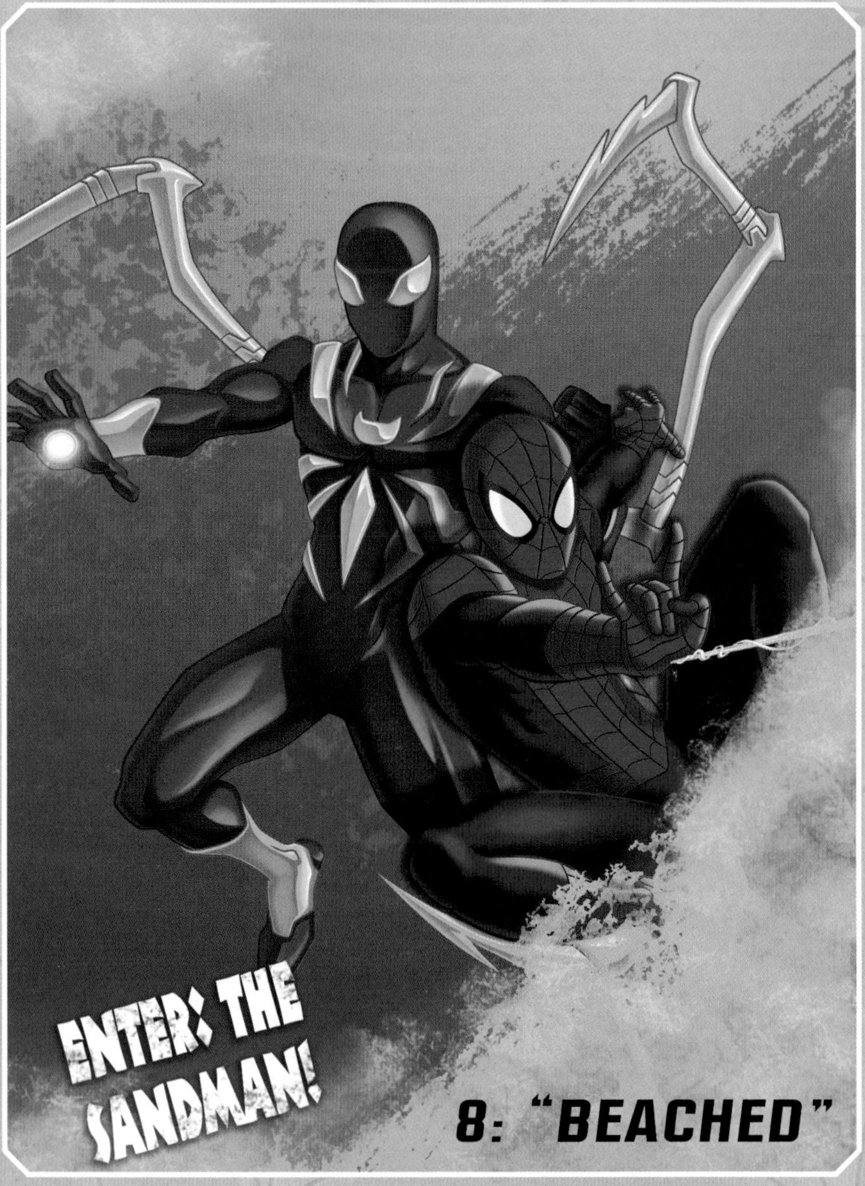
ENTER: THE SANDMAN!
8: "BEACHED"

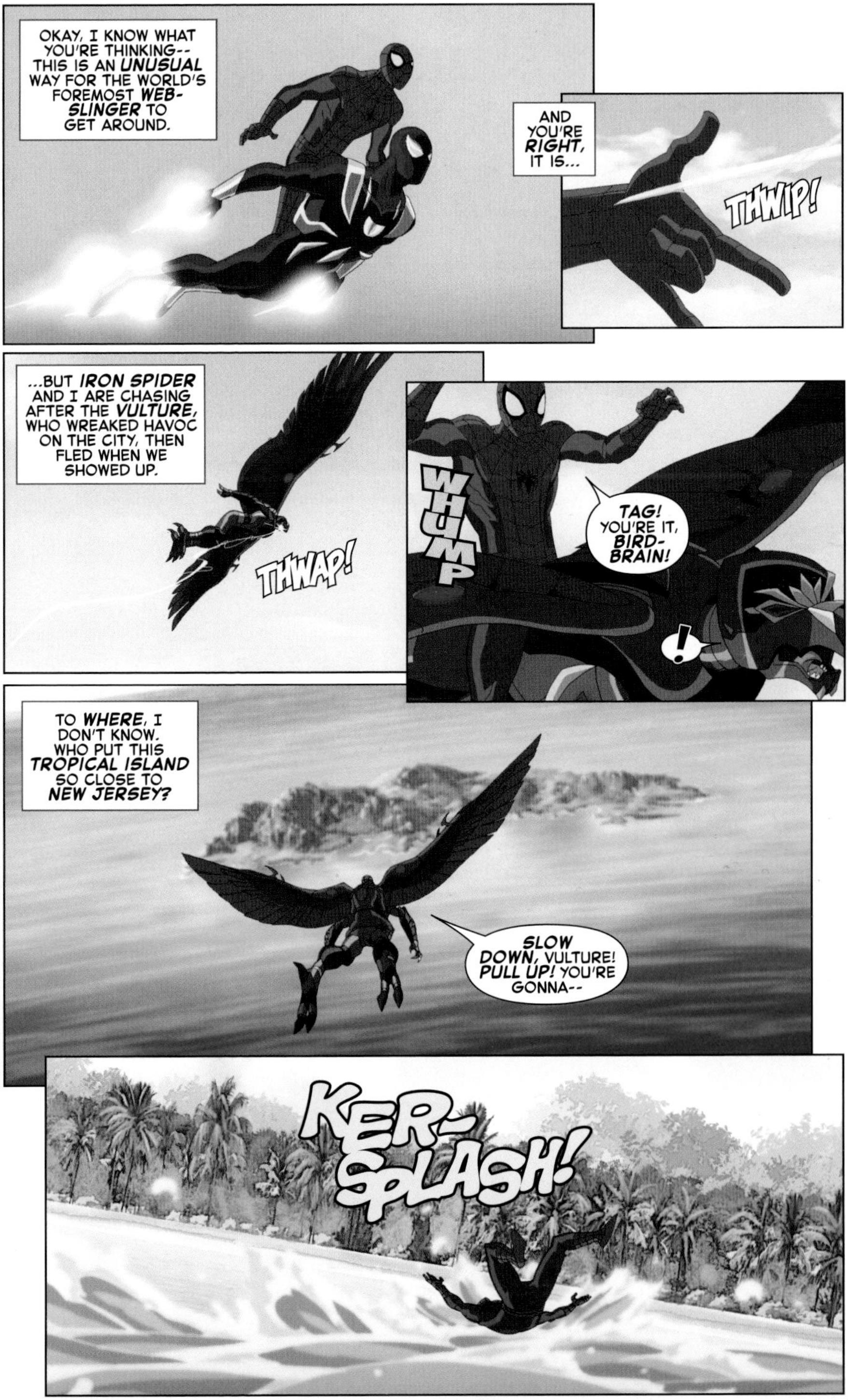
OKAY, I KNOW WHAT YOU'RE THINKING-- THIS IS AN UNUSUAL WAY FOR THE WORLD'S FOREMOST WEB-SLINGER TO GET AROUND.
AND YOU'RE RIGHT, IT IS...
THWIP!
...BUT IRON SPIDER AND I ARE CHASING AFTER THE VULTURE, WHO WREAKED HAVOC ON THE CITY, THEN FLED WHEN WE SHOWED UP.
THWAP!
WHUMP
TAG! YOU'RE IT, BIRD-BRAIN!
!
TO WHERE, I DON'T KNOW. WHO PUT THIS TROPICAL ISLAND SO CLOSE TO NEW JERSEY?
SLOW DOWN, VULTURE! PULL UP! YOU'RE GONNA--
KER-SPLASH!

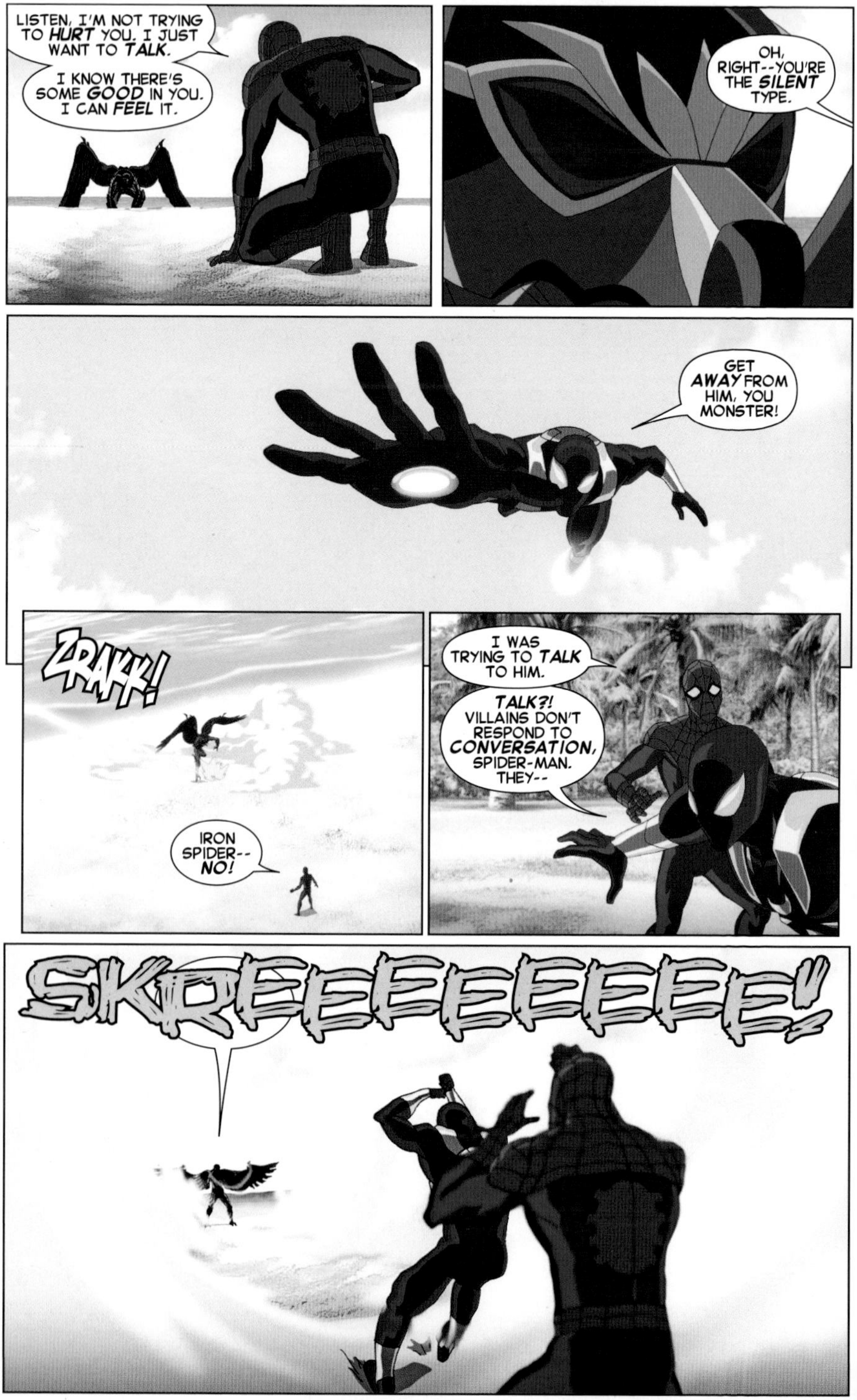
LISTEN, I'M NOT TRYING TO HURT YOU. I JUST WANT TO TALK.
I KNOW THERE'S SOME GOOD IN YOU. I CAN FEEL IT.
OH, RIGHT--YOU'RE THE SILENT TYPE.
GET AWAY FROM HIM, YOU MONSTER!
ZRAKK!
IRON SPIDER--NO!
I WAS TRYING TO TALK TO HIM.
TALK?! VILLAINS DON'T RESPOND TO CONVERSATION, SPIDER-MAN. THEY--
SKREEEEEEEEEE!

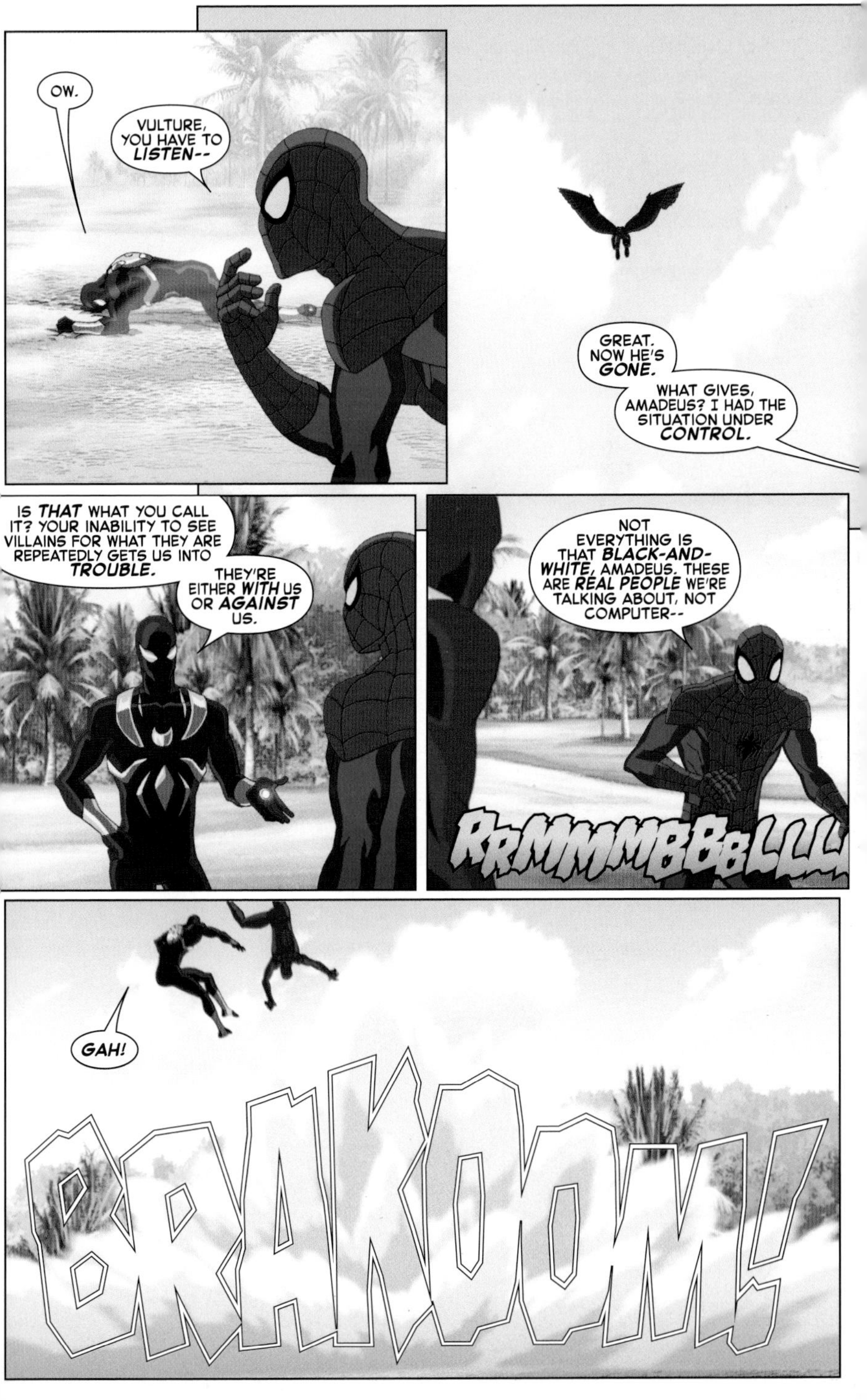

OW.
VULTURE, YOU HAVE TO LISTEN--
GREAT. NOW HE'S GONE.
WHAT GIVES, AMADEUS? I HAD THE SITUATION UNDER CONTROL.
IS THAT WHAT YOU CALL IT? YOUR INABILITY TO SEE VILLAINS FOR WHAT THEY ARE REPEATEDLY GETS US INTO TROUBLE.
THEY'RE EITHER WITH US OR AGAINST US.
NOT EVERYTHING IS THAT BLACK-AND-WHITE, AMADEUS. THESE ARE REAL PEOPLE WE'RE TALKING ABOUT, NOT COMPUTER--
RRMMMMBBBLLLL
GAH!
CRAKOOM!

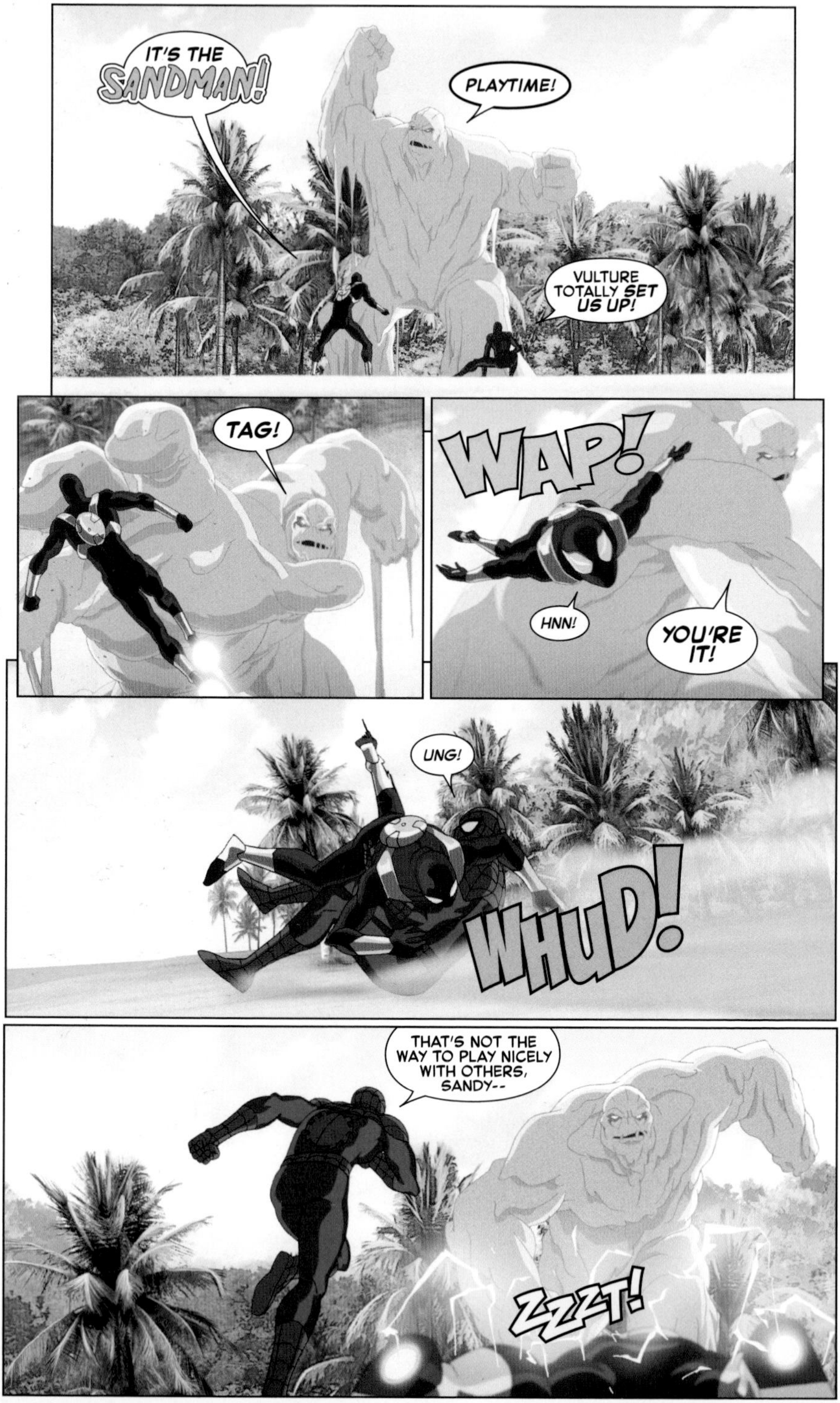
IT'S THE SANDMAN!
PLAYTIME!
VULTURE TOTALLY SET US UP!
TAG!
WAP!
HNN!
YOU'RE IT!
UNG!
WHUD!
THAT'S NOT THE WAY TO PLAY NICELY WITH OTHERS, SANDY--
ZZZT!

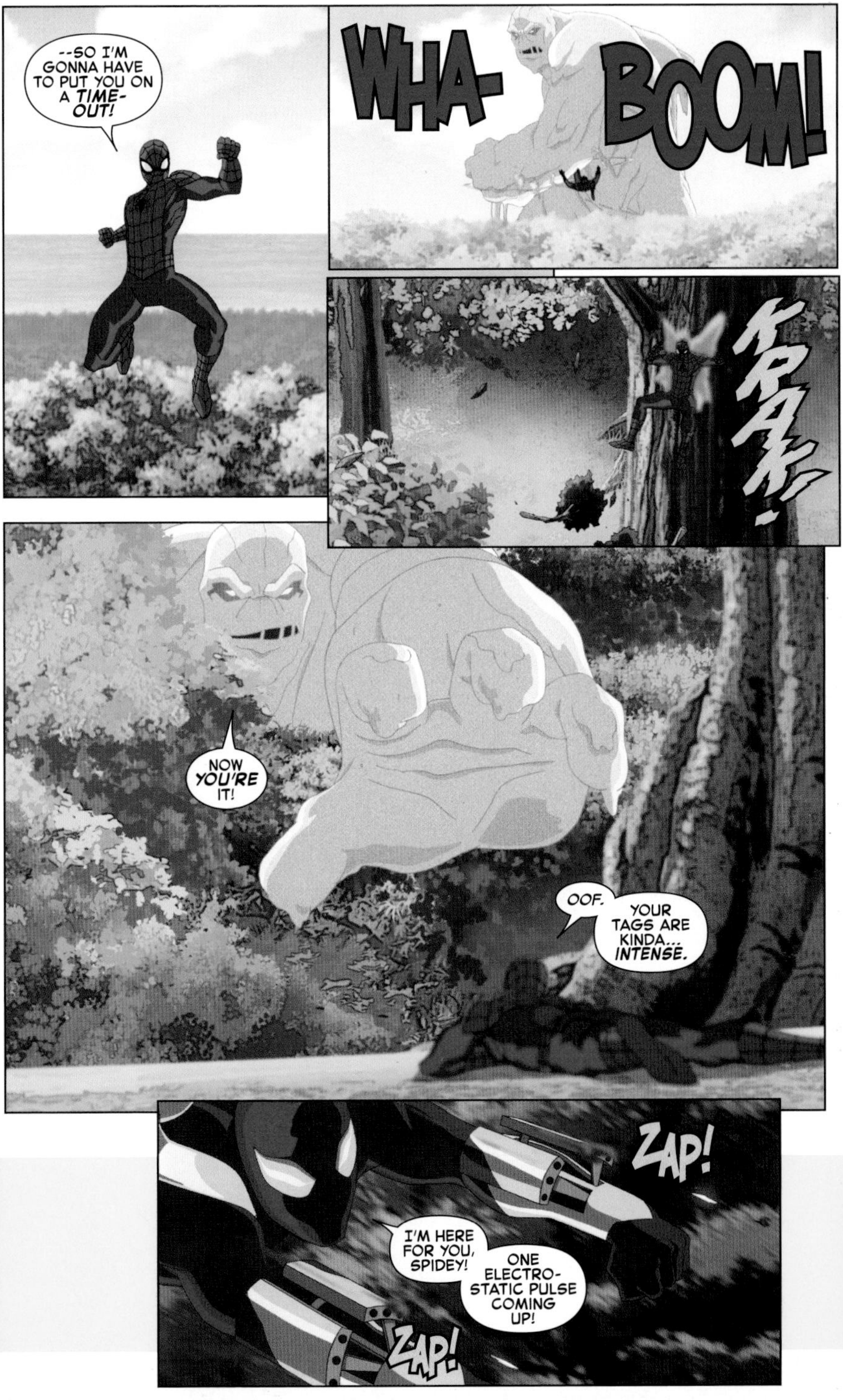
--SO I'M GONNA HAVE TO PUT YOU ON A TIME-OUT!
WHA-BOOM!
KRAK!
NOW YOU'RE IT!
OOF.
YOUR TAGS ARE KINDA... INTENSE.
ZAP!
I'M HERE FOR YOU, SPIDEY!
ONE ELECTRO-STATIC PULSE COMING UP!
ZAP!

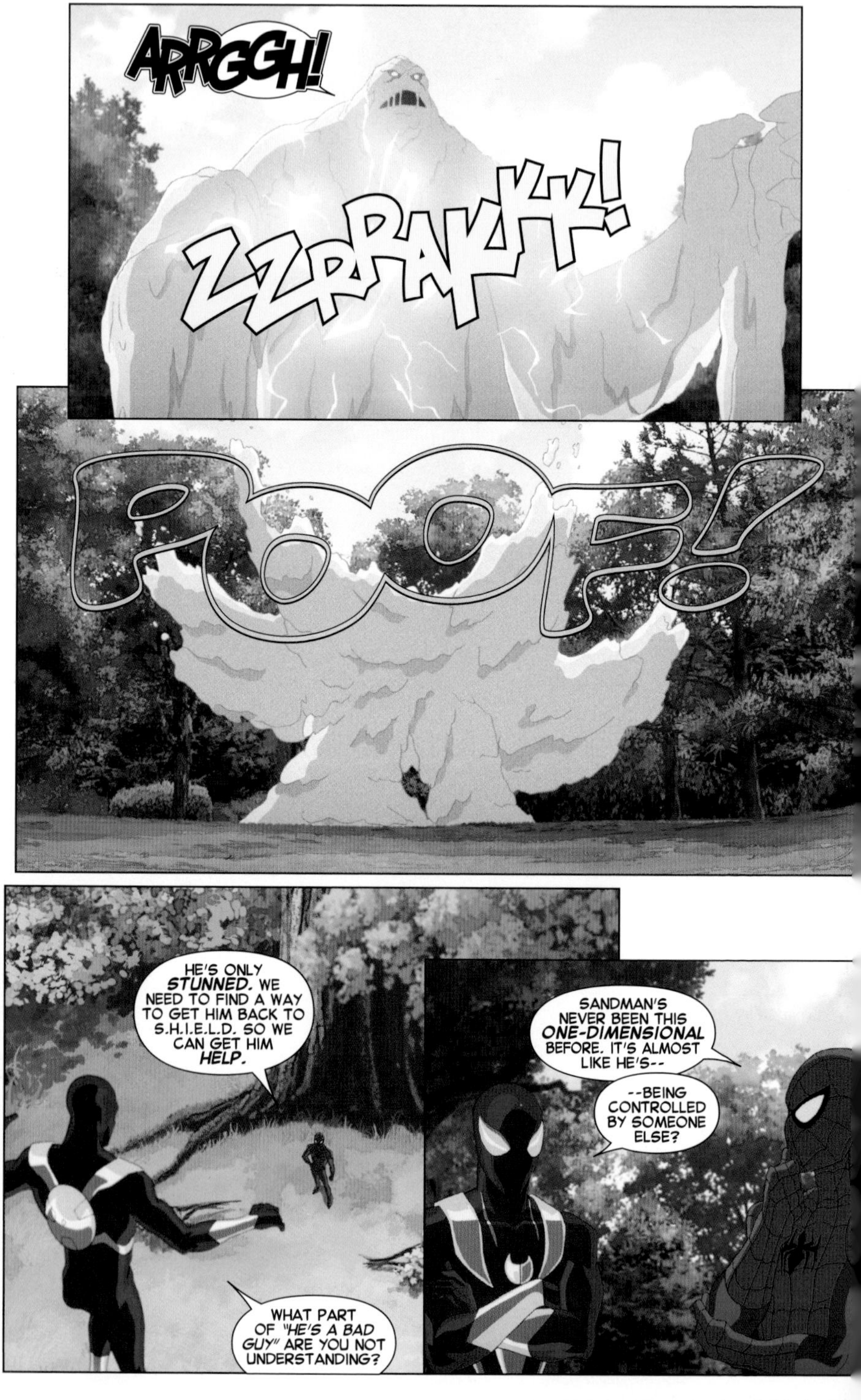
ARRGGH!
ZZRRAKKK!
POOF!
HE'S ONLY STUNNED. WE NEED TO FIND A WAY TO GET HIM BACK TO S.H.I.E.L.D. SO WE CAN GET HIM HELP.
WHAT PART OF "HE'S A BAD GUY" ARE YOU NOT UNDERSTANDING?
SANDMAN'S NEVER BEEN THIS ONE-DIMENSIONAL BEFORE. IT'S ALMOST LIKE HE'S--
--BEING CONTROLLED BY SOMEONE ELSE?

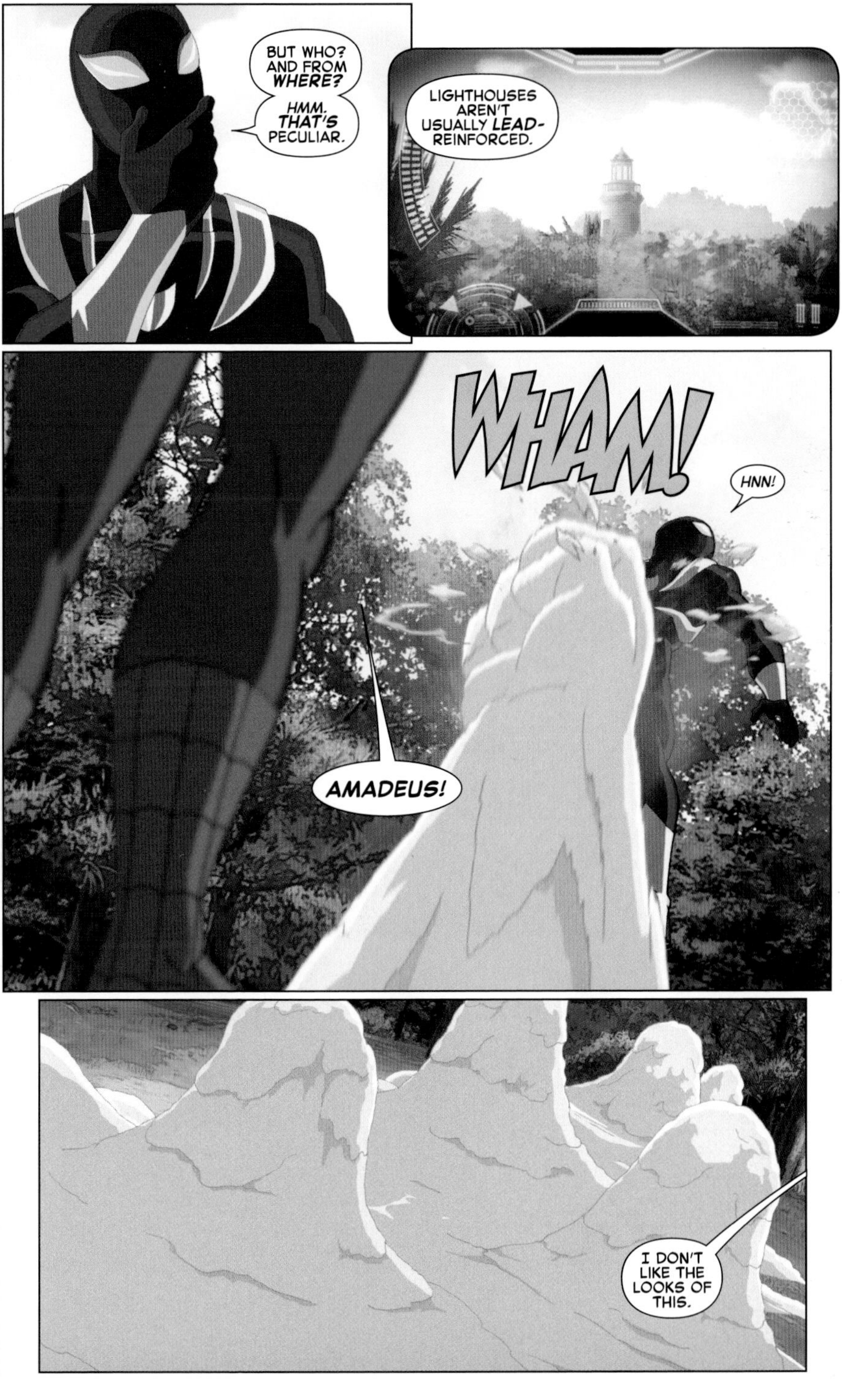
BUT WHO? AND FROM WHERE?
HMM. THAT'S PECULIAR.
LIGHTHOUSES AREN'T USUALLY LEAD-REINFORCED.
WHAM!
HNN!
AMADEUS!
I DON'T LIKE THE LOOKS OF THIS.

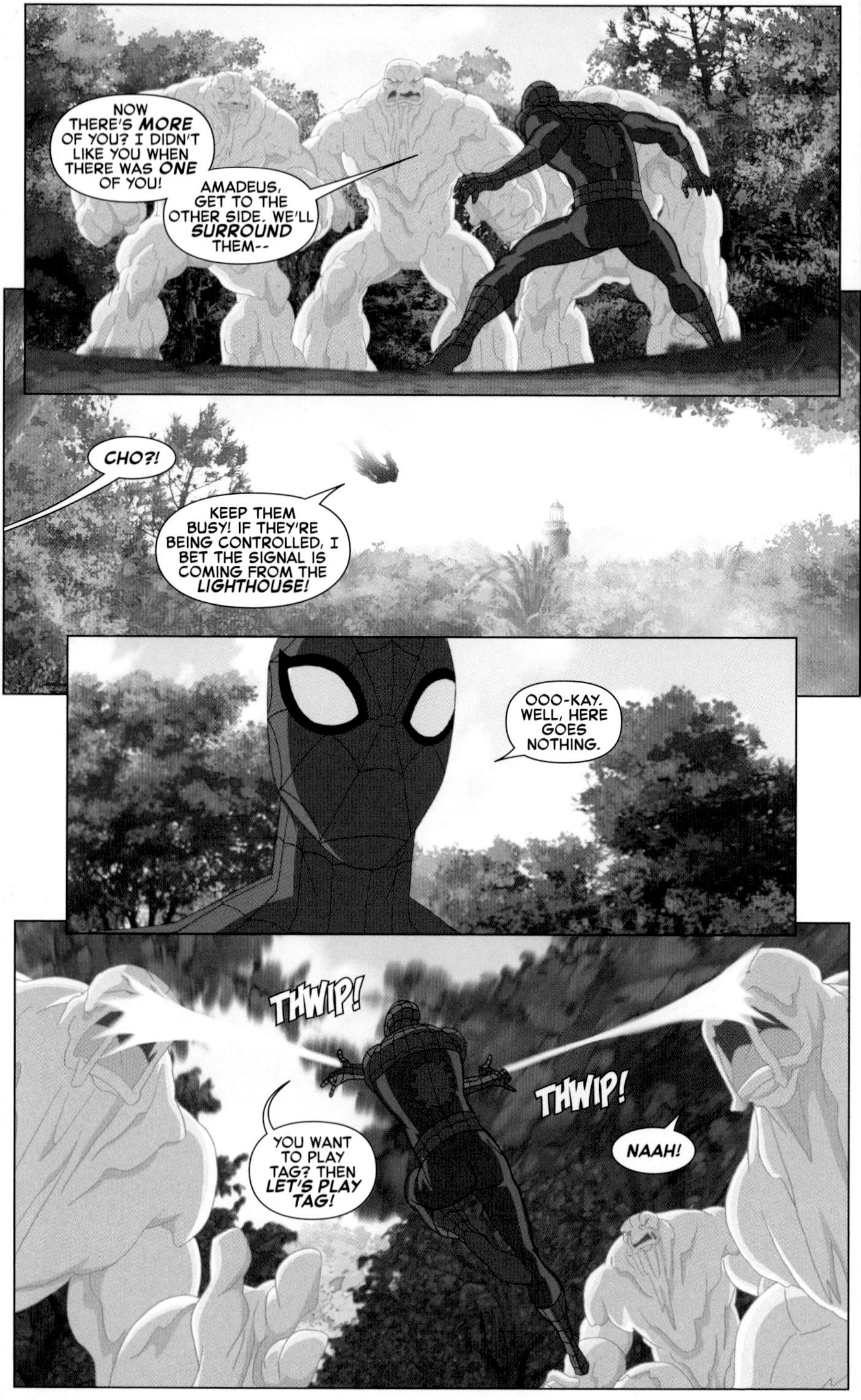
NOW THERE'S MORE OF YOU? I DIDN'T LIKE YOU WHEN THERE WAS ONE OF YOU!
AMADEUS, GET TO THE OTHER SIDE. WE'LL SURROUND THEM--
CHO?!
KEEP THEM BUSY! IF THEY'RE BEING CONTROLLED, I BET THE SIGNAL IS COMING FROM THE LIGHTHOUSE!
OOO-KAY. WELL, HERE GOES NOTHING.
THWIP!
YOU WANT TO PLAY TAG? THEN LET'S PLAY TAG!
THWIP!
NAAH!

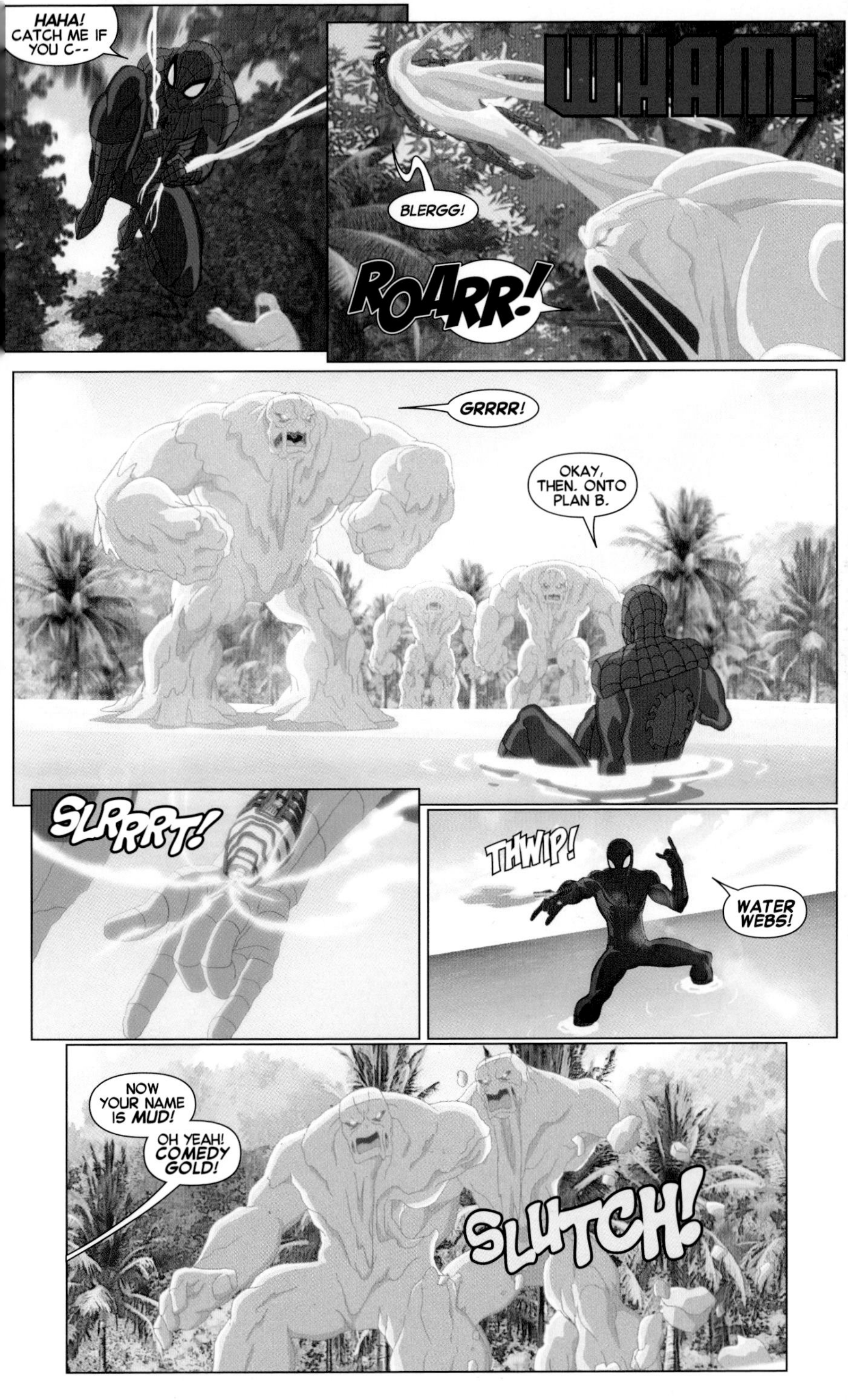
HAHA! CATCH ME IF YOU C--
WHAM!
BLERGG!
ROARR!
GRRRR!
OKAY, THEN. ONTO PLAN B.
SLRRRT!
THWIP!
WATER WEBS!
NOW YOUR NAME IS MUD!
OH YEAH! COMEDY GOLD!
SLUTCH!

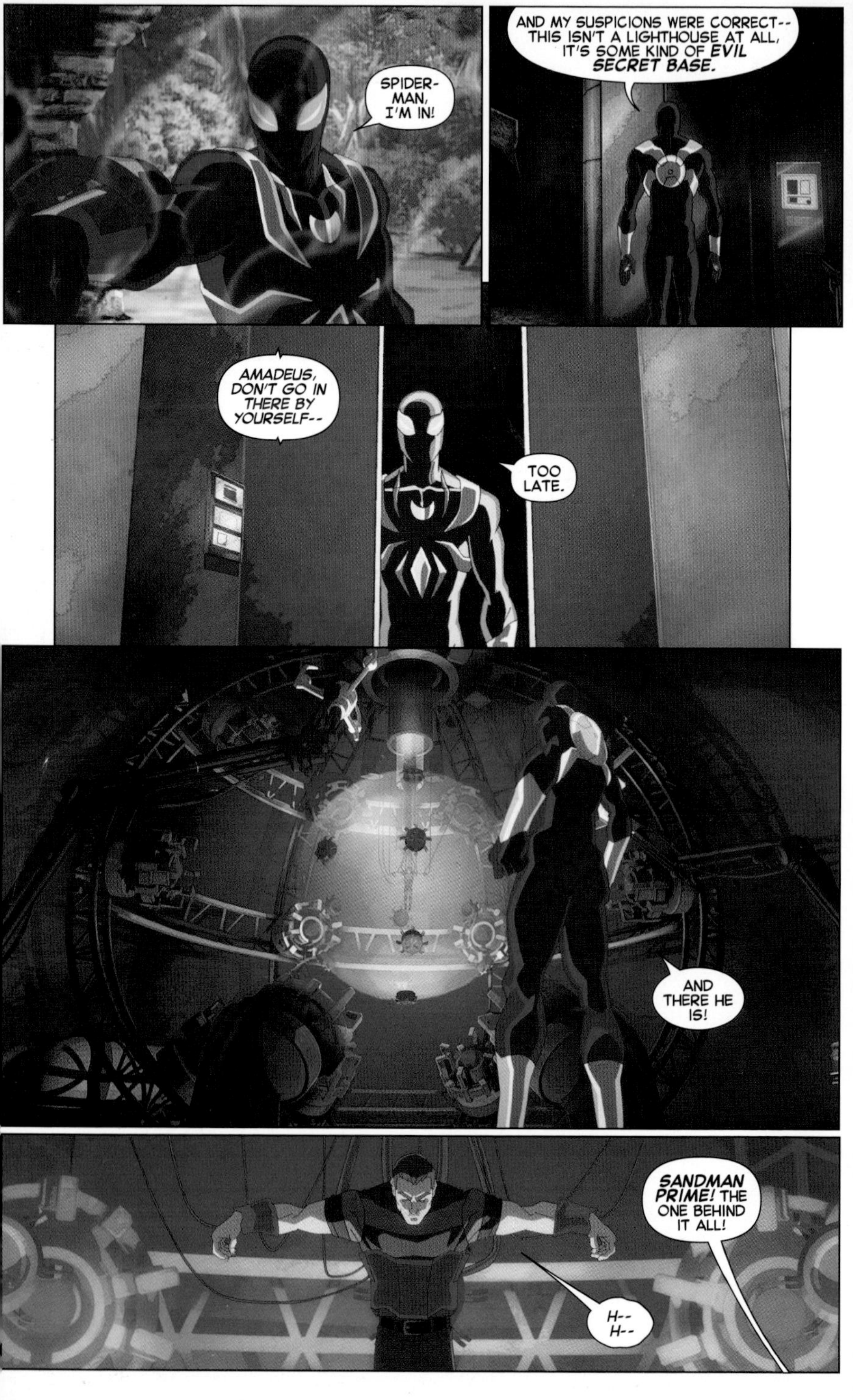
SPIDER-MAN, I'M IN!
AND MY SUSPICIONS WERE CORRECT-- THIS ISN'T A LIGHTHOUSE AT ALL, IT'S SOME KIND OF EVIL SECRET BASE.
AMADEUS, DON'T GO IN THERE BY YOURSELF--
TOO LATE.
AND THERE HE IS!
SANDMAN PRIME! THE ONE BEHIND IT ALL!
H-- H--

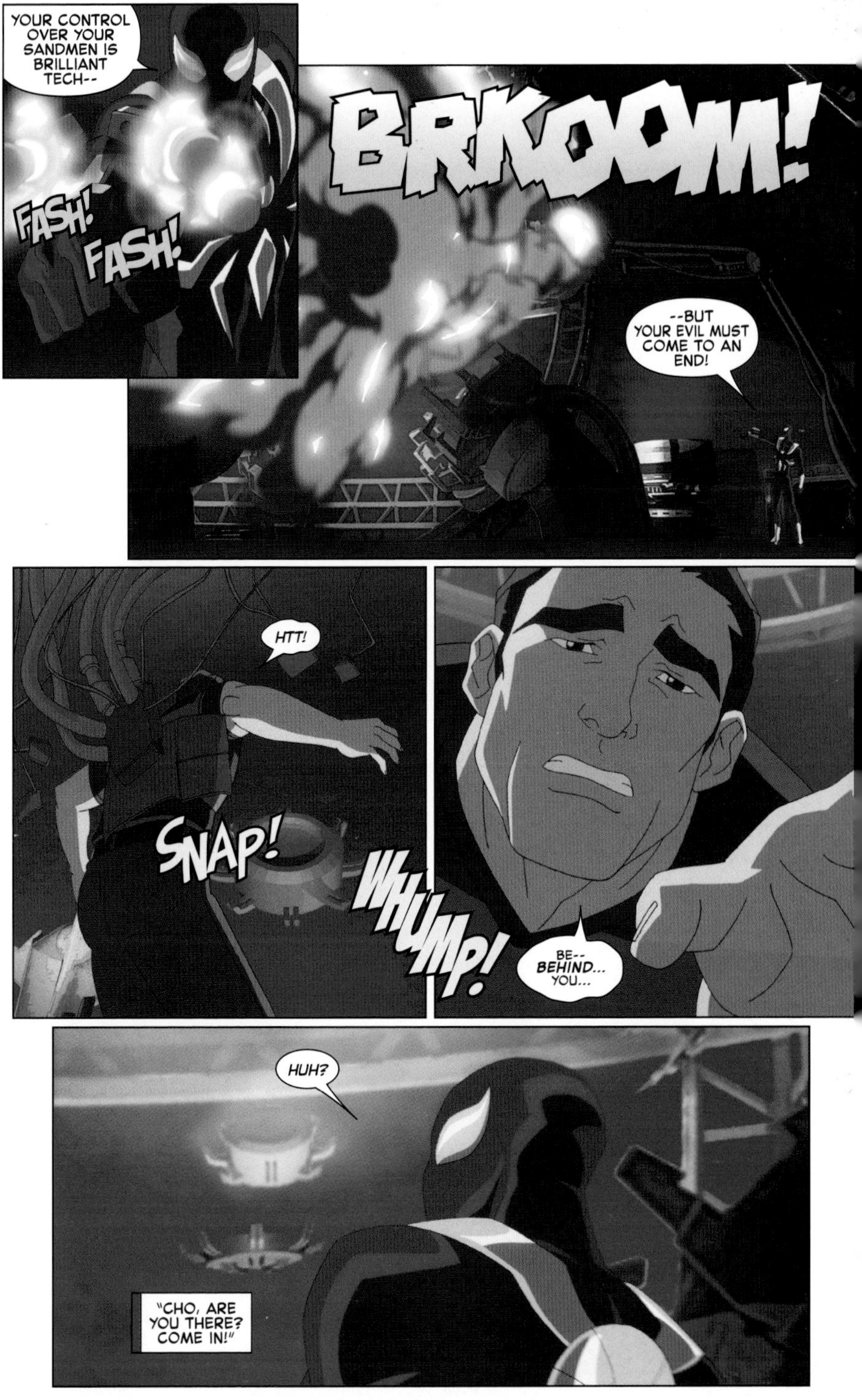
YOUR CONTROL OVER YOUR SANDMEN IS BRILLIANT TECH--
FASH! FASH!
BRKOOM!
--BUT YOUR EVIL MUST COME TO AN END!
HTT!
SNAP!
WHUMP!
BE-- BEHIND... YOU...
HUH?
"CHO, ARE YOU THERE? COME IN!"

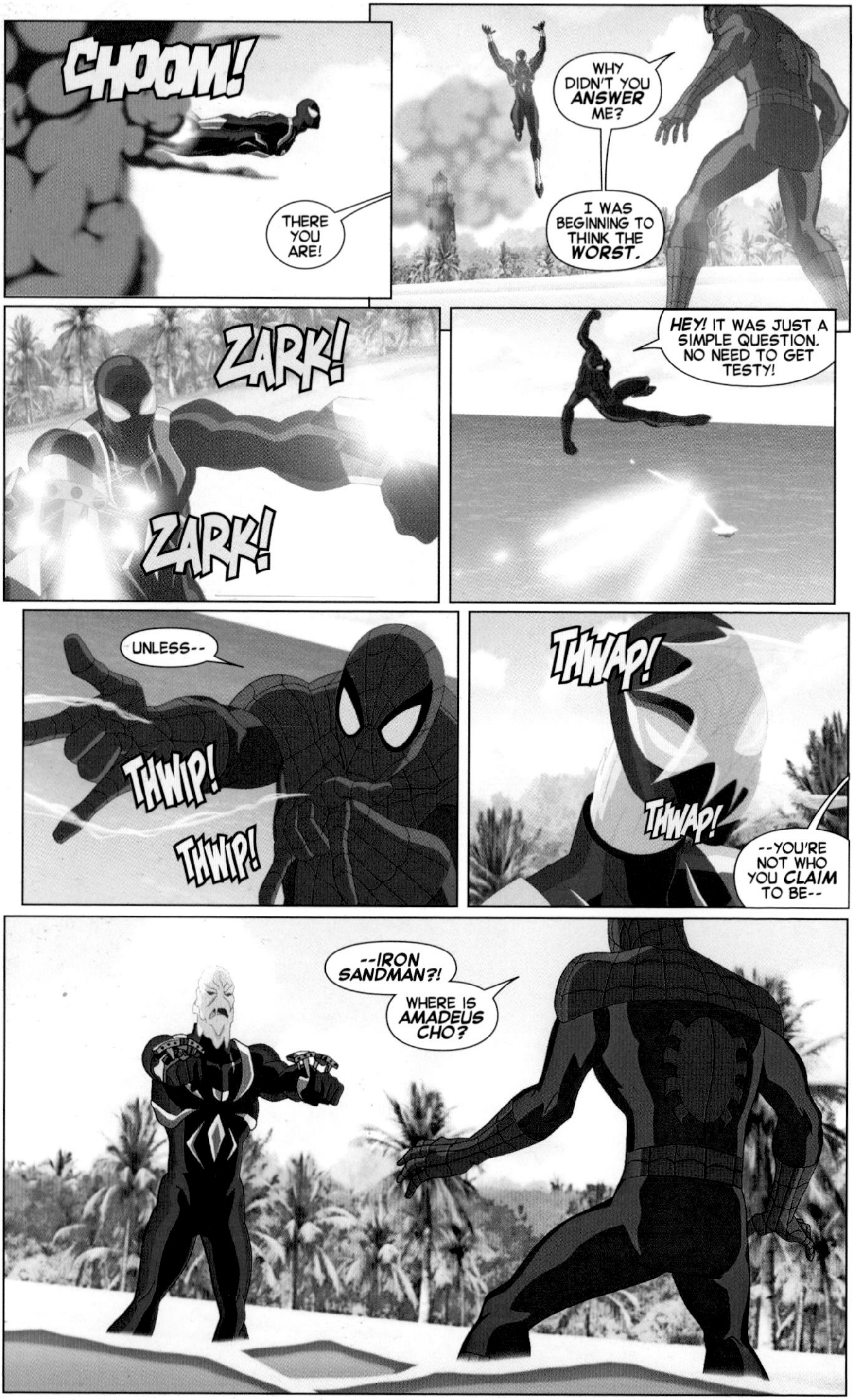
CHOOM!
THERE YOU ARE!
WHY DIDN'T YOU ANSWER ME?
I WAS BEGINNING TO THINK THE WORST.
ZARK!
ZARK!
HEY! IT WAS JUST A SIMPLE QUESTION. NO NEED TO GET TESTY!
UNLESS--
THWIP!
THWIP!
THWAP!
THWAP!
--YOU'RE NOT WHO YOU CLAIM TO BE--
--IRON SANDMAN?!
WHERE IS AMADEUS CHO?

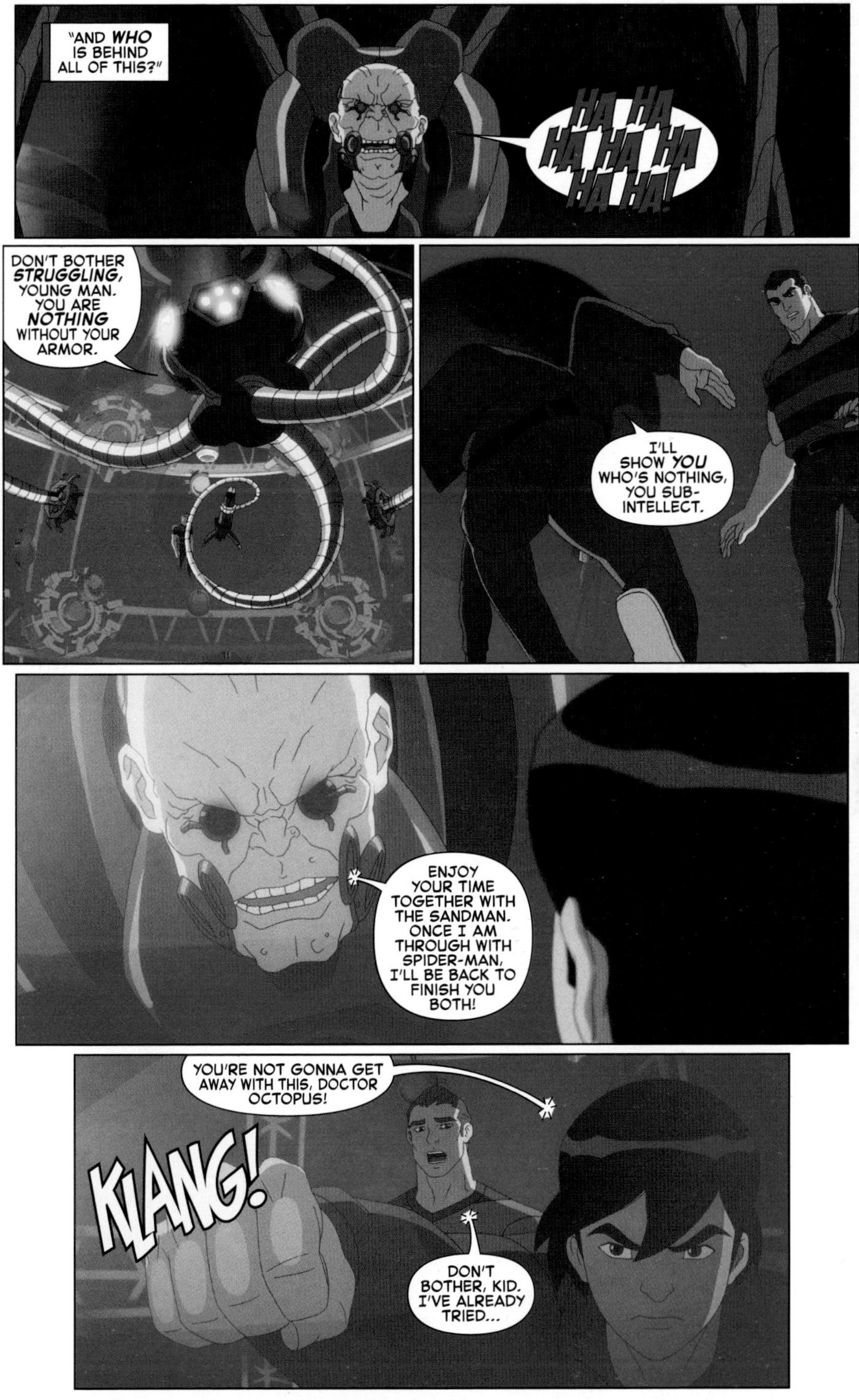
"AND WHO IS BEHIND ALL OF THIS?"
HA HA HA HA HA HA HA!
DON'T BOTHER STRUGGLING, YOUNG MAN. YOU ARE NOTHING WITHOUT YOUR ARMOR.
I'LL SHOW YOU WHO'S NOTHING, YOU SUB-INTELLECT.
ENJOY YOUR TIME TOGETHER WITH THE SANDMAN. ONCE I AM THROUGH WITH SPIDER-MAN, I'LL BE BACK TO FINISH YOU BOTH!
YOU'RE NOT GONNA GET AWAY WITH THIS, DOCTOR OCTOPUS!
KLANG!
DON'T BOTHER, KID. I'VE ALREADY TRIED...

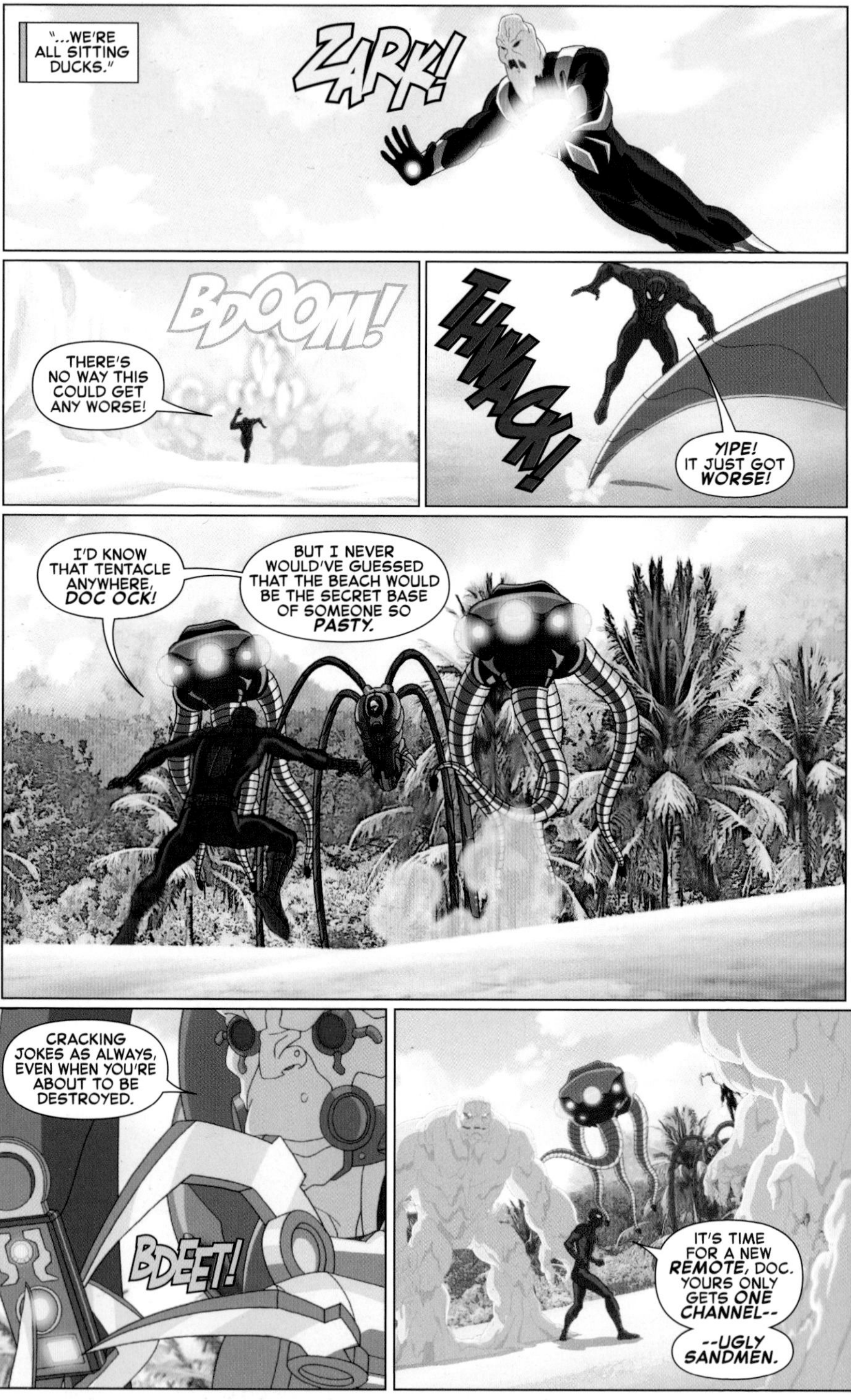

"...WE'RE ALL SITTING DUCKS."
ZARK!
BDOOM!
THERE'S NO WAY THIS COULD GET ANY WORSE!
THWACK!
YIPE! IT JUST GOT WORSE!
I'D KNOW THAT TENTACLE ANYWHERE, DOC OCK!
BUT I NEVER WOULD'VE GUESSED THAT THE BEACH WOULD BE THE SECRET BASE OF SOMEONE SO PASTY.
CRACKING JOKES AS ALWAYS, EVEN WHEN YOU'RE ABOUT TO BE DESTROYED.
BDEET!
IT'S TIME FOR A NEW REMOTE, DOC. YOURS ONLY GETS ONE CHANNEL--
--UGLY SANDMEN.

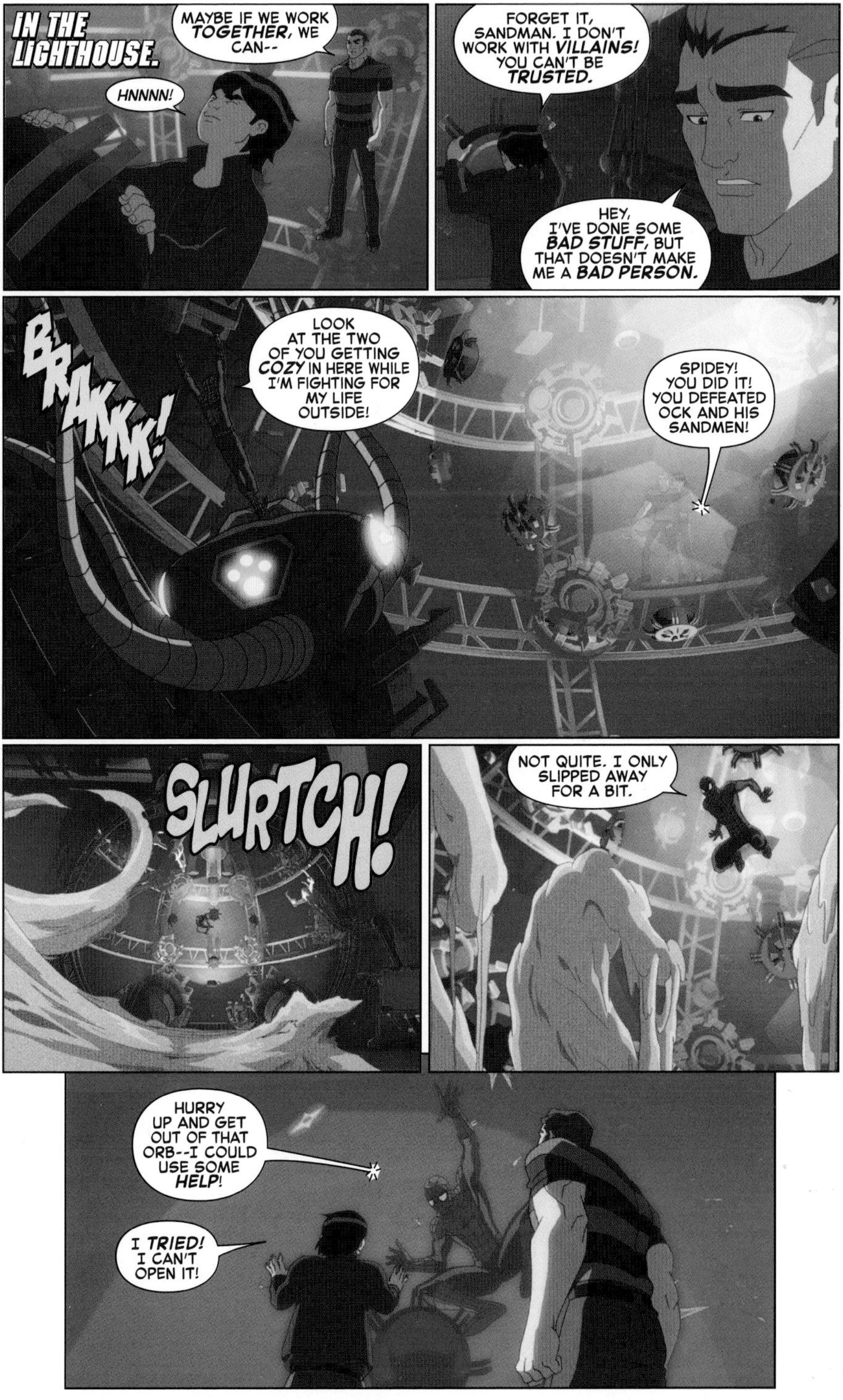
IN THE LIGHTHOUSE.
MAYBE IF WE WORK TOGETHER, WE CAN--
HNNNN!
FORGET IT, SANDMAN. I DON'T WORK WITH VILLAINS! YOU CAN'T BE TRUSTED.
HEY, I'VE DONE SOME BAD STUFF, BUT THAT DOESN'T MAKE ME A BAD PERSON.
BRAKKKK!
LOOK AT THE TWO OF YOU GETTING COZY IN HERE WHILE I'M FIGHTING FOR MY LIFE OUTSIDE!
SPIDEY! YOU DID IT! YOU DEFEATED OCK AND HIS SANDMEN!
SLURTCH!
NOT QUITE. I ONLY SLIPPED AWAY FOR A BIT.
HURRY UP AND GET OUT OF THAT ORB--I COULD USE SOME HELP!
I TRIED! I CAN'T OPEN IT!

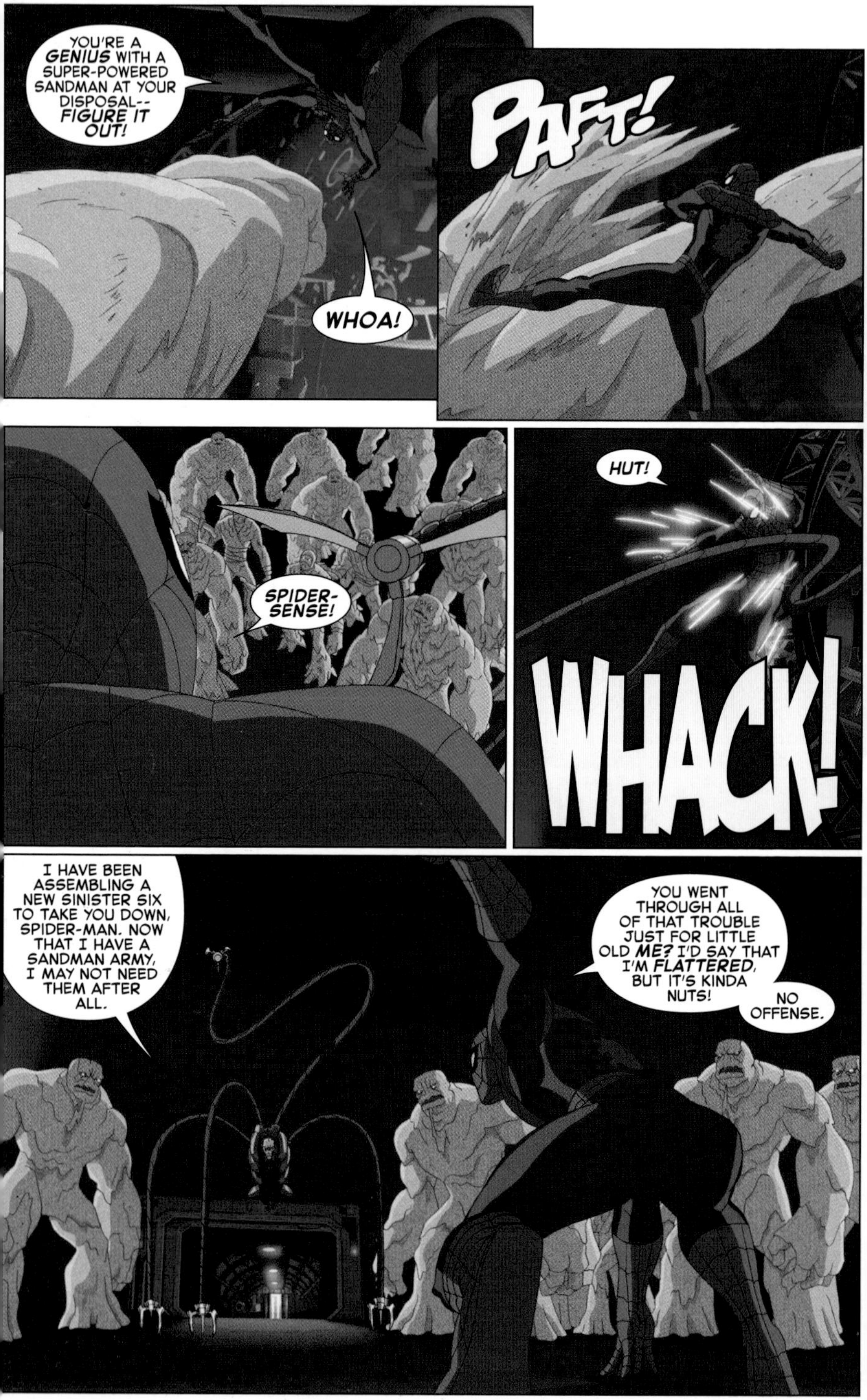
YOU'RE A GENIUS WITH A SUPER-POWERED SANDMAN AT YOUR DISPOSAL-- FIGURE IT OUT!
WHOA!
PAFT!
SPIDER-SENSE!
HUT!
WHACK!
I HAVE BEEN ASSEMBLING A NEW SINISTER SIX TO TAKE YOU DOWN, SPIDER-MAN. NOW THAT I HAVE A SANDMAN ARMY, I MAY NOT NEED THEM AFTER ALL.
YOU WENT THROUGH ALL OF THAT TROUBLE JUST FOR LITTLE OLD ME? I'D SAY THAT I'M FLATTERED, BUT IT'S KINDA NUTS!
NO OFFENSE.

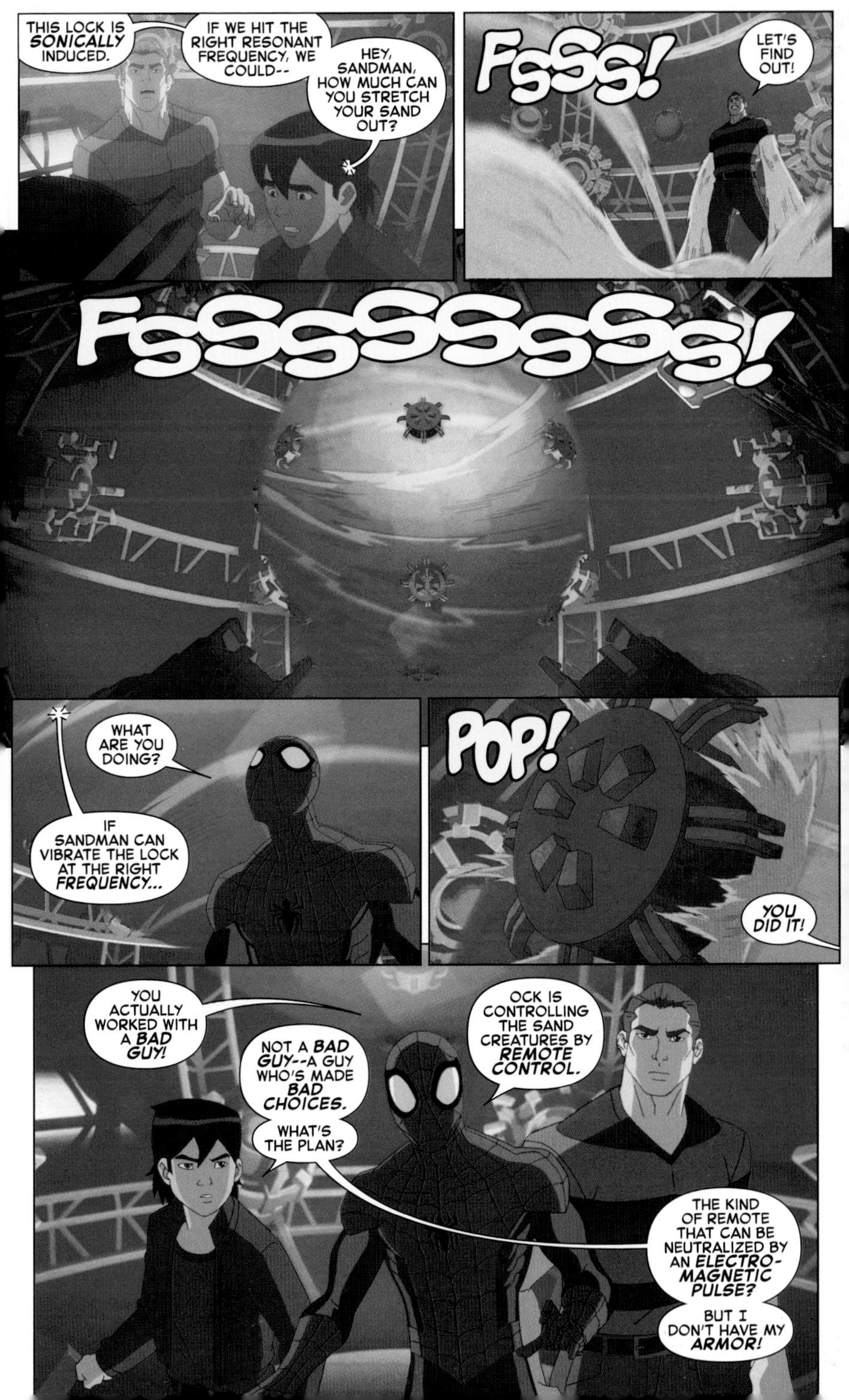

THIS LOCK IS SONICALLY INDUCED.
IF WE HIT THE RIGHT RESONANT FREQUENCY, WE COULD--
HEY, SANDMAN, HOW MUCH CAN YOU STRETCH YOUR SAND OUT?
FSSS!
LET'S FIND OUT!
FSSSSSSSS!
WHAT ARE YOU DOING?
IF SANDMAN CAN VIBRATE THE LOCK AT THE RIGHT FREQUENCY...
POP!
YOU DID IT!
YOU ACTUALLY WORKED WITH A BAD GUY!
NOT A BAD GUY--A GUY WHO'S MADE BAD CHOICES.
WHAT'S THE PLAN?
OCK IS CONTROLLING THE SAND CREATURES BY REMOTE CONTROL.
THE KIND OF REMOTE THAT CAN BE NEUTRALIZED BY AN ELECTRO-MAGNETIC PULSE?
BUT I DON'T HAVE MY ARMOR!

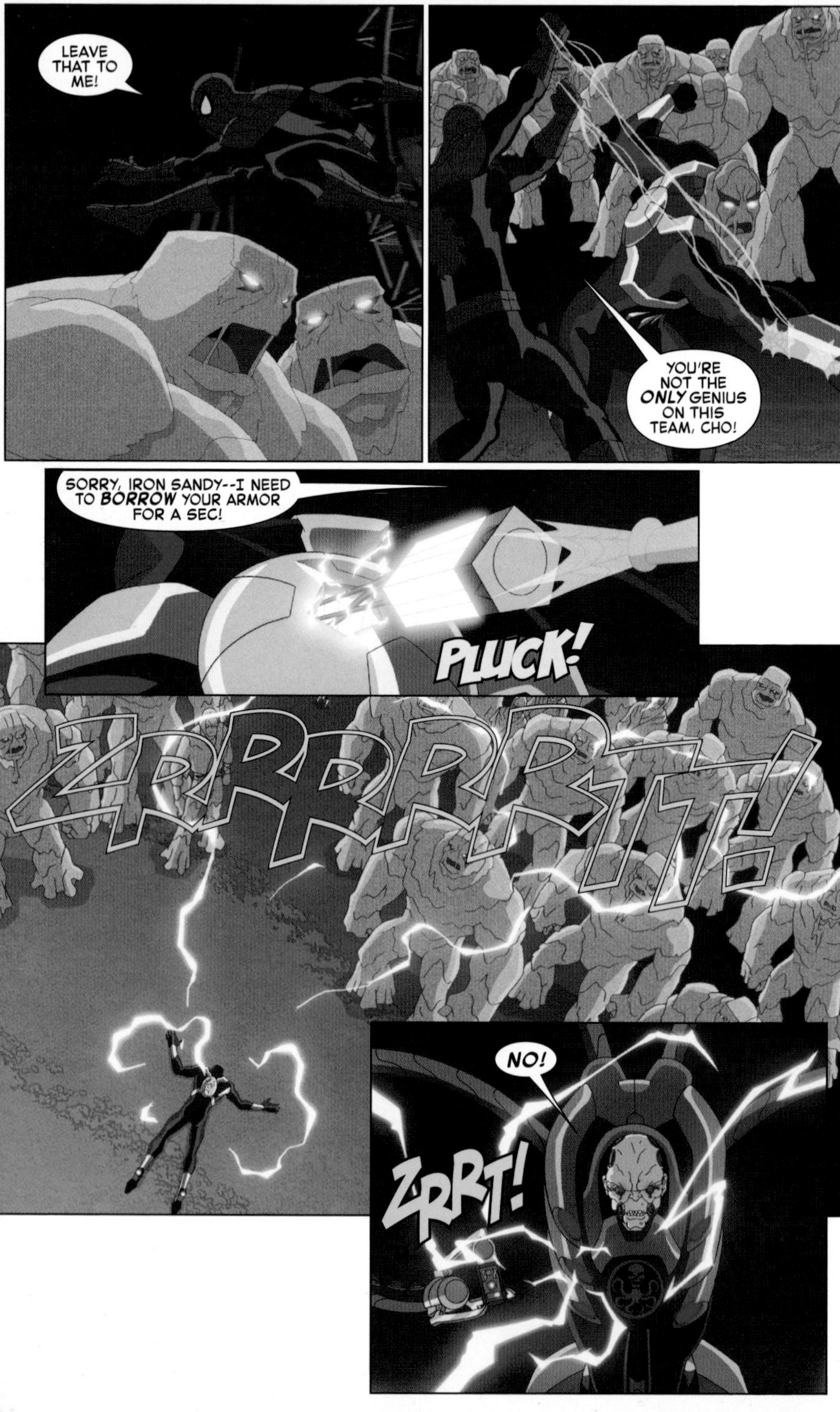
LEAVE THAT TO ME!
YOU'RE NOT THE ONLY GENIUS ON THIS TEAM, CHO!
SORRY, IRON SANDY--I NEED TO BORROW YOUR ARMOR FOR A SEC!
PLUCK!
ZRRRRRTT!
NO!
ZRRT!

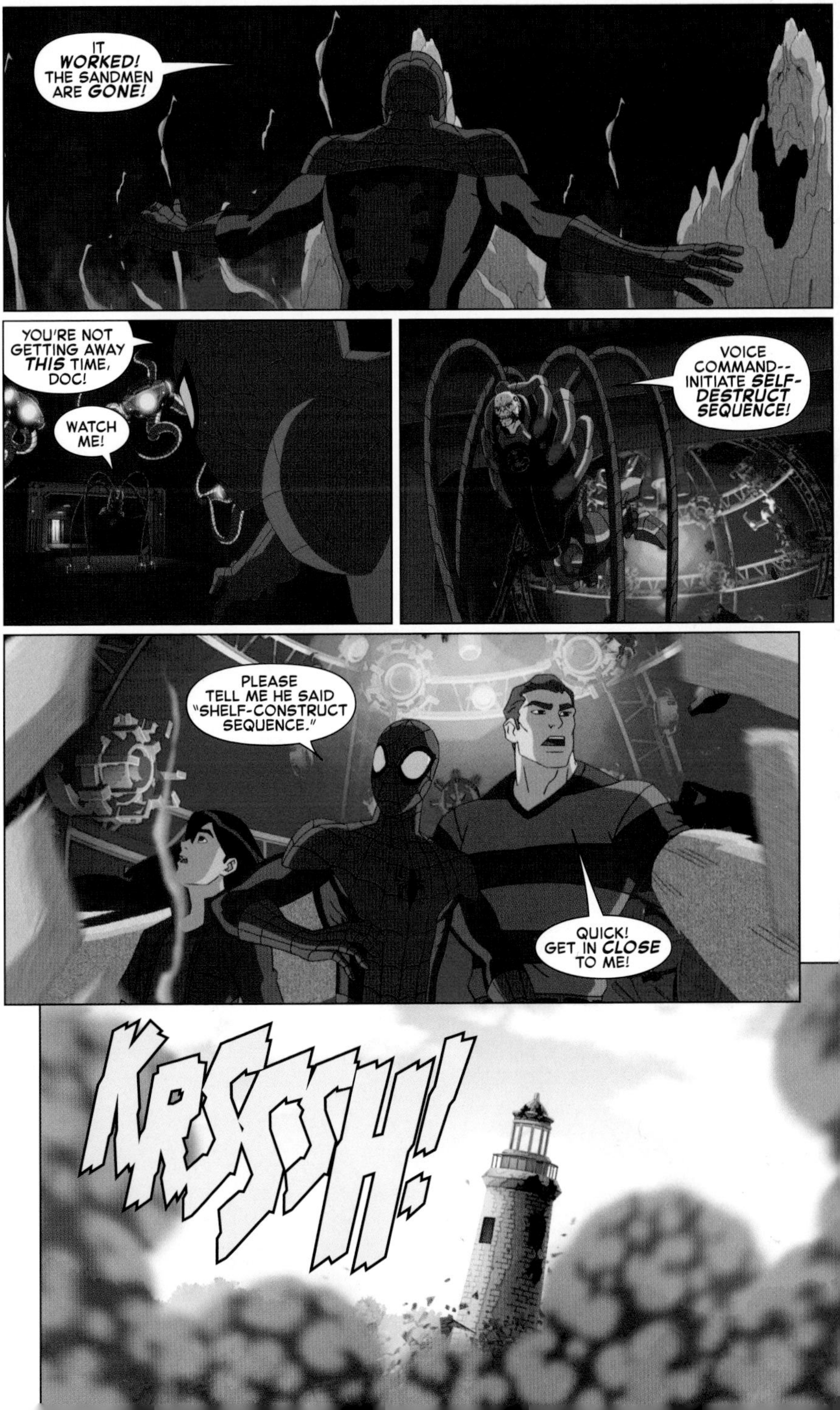
IT WORKED! THE SANDMEN ARE GONE!
YOU'RE NOT GETTING AWAY THIS TIME, DOC!
WATCH ME!
VOICE COMMAND-- INITIATE SELF-DESTRUCT SEQUENCE!
PLEASE TELL ME HE SAID "SHELF-CONSTRUCT SEQUENCE."
QUICK! GET IN CLOSE TO ME!
KRSSSH!

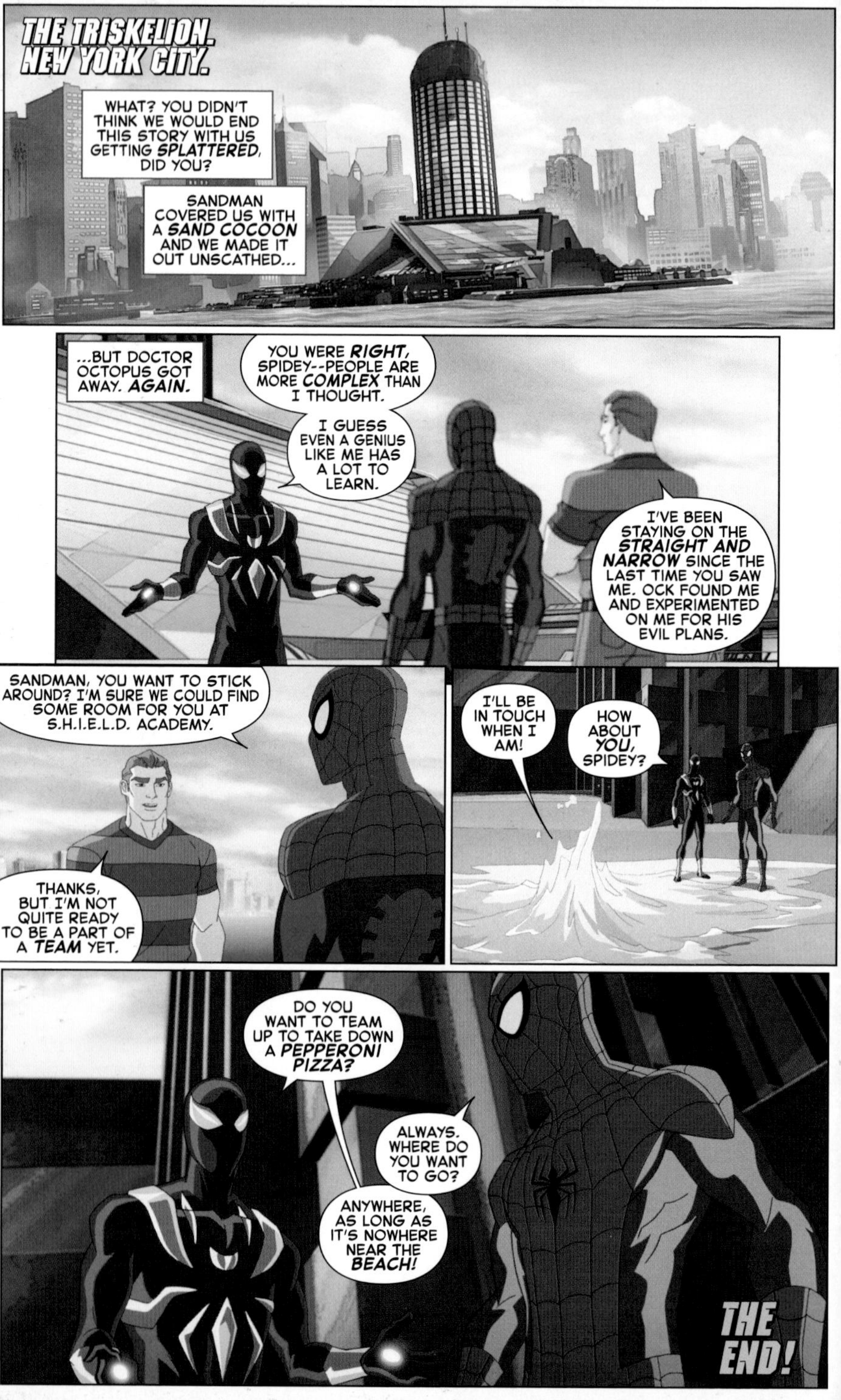
THE TRISKELION. NEW YORK CITY.
WHAT? YOU DIDN'T THINK WE WOULD END THIS STORY WITH US GETTING SPLATTERED, DID YOU?
SANDMAN COVERED US WITH A SAND COCOON AND WE MADE IT OUT UNSCATHED...
...BUT DOCTOR OCTOPUS GOT AWAY. AGAIN.
YOU WERE RIGHT, SPIDEY--PEOPLE ARE MORE COMPLEX THAN I THOUGHT.
I GUESS EVEN A GENIUS LIKE ME HAS A LOT TO LEARN.
I'VE BEEN STAYING ON THE STRAIGHT AND NARROW SINCE THE LAST TIME YOU SAW ME. OCK FOUND ME AND EXPERIMENTED ON ME FOR HIS EVIL PLANS.
SANDMAN, YOU WANT TO STICK AROUND? I'M SURE WE COULD FIND SOME ROOM FOR YOU AT S.H.I.E.L.D. ACADEMY.
THANKS, BUT I'M NOT QUITE READY TO BE A PART OF A TEAM YET.
I'LL BE IN TOUCH WHEN I AM!
HOW ABOUT YOU, SPIDEY?
DO YOU WANT TO TEAM UP TO TAKE DOWN A PEPPERONI PIZZA?
ALWAYS. WHERE DO YOU WANT TO GO?
ANYWHERE, AS LONG AS IT'S NOWHERE NEAR THE BEACH!
THE END!

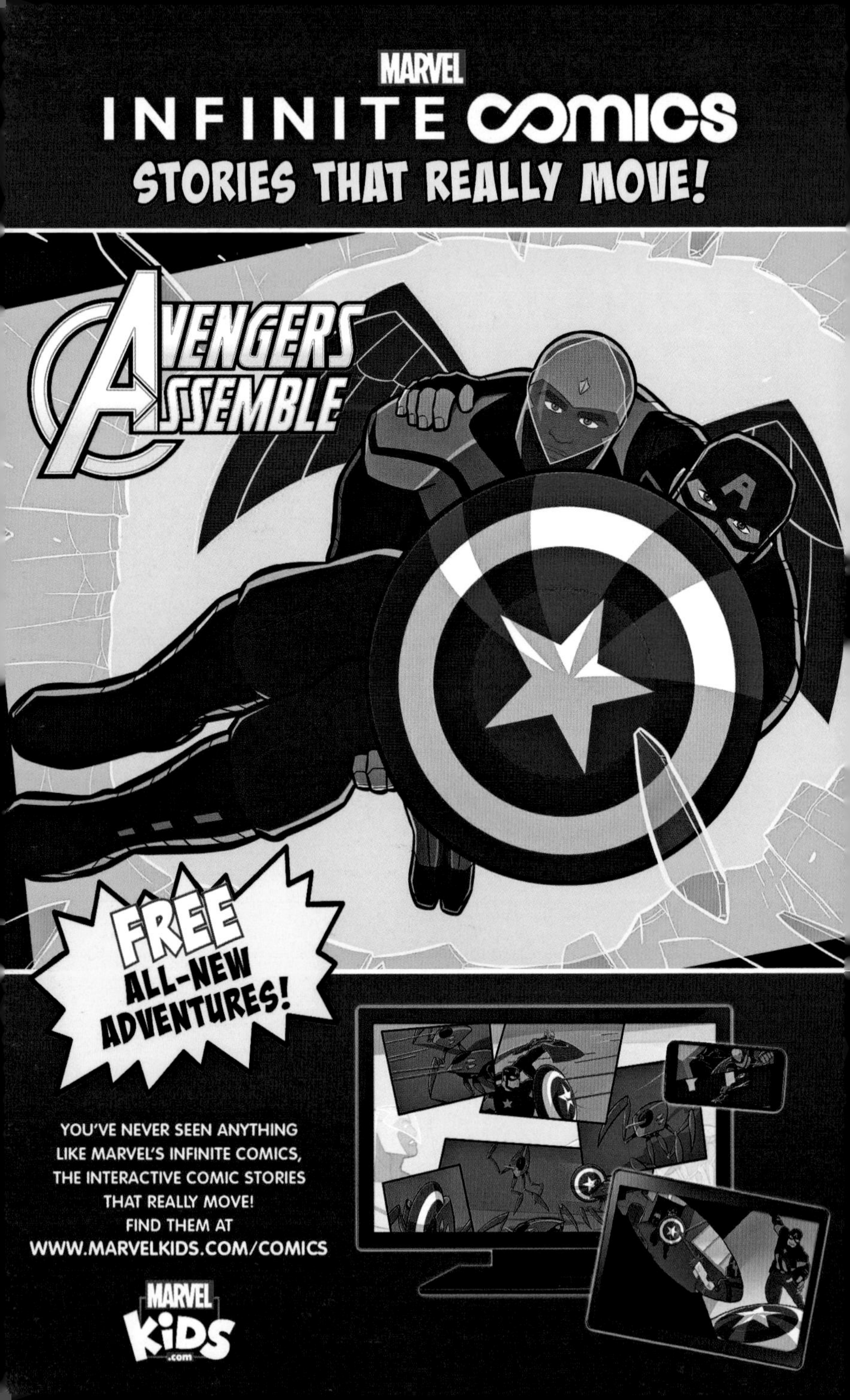
MARVEL
INFINITE COMICS
STORIES THAT REALLY MOVE!
AVENGERS ASSEMBLE
FREE ALL-NEW ADVENTURES!
YOU'VE NEVER SEEN ANYTHING LIKE MARVEL'S INFINITE COMICS, THE INTERACTIVE COMIC STORIES THAT REALLY MOVE! FIND THEM AT WWW.MARVELKIDS.COM/COMICS
MARVEL KIDS .com

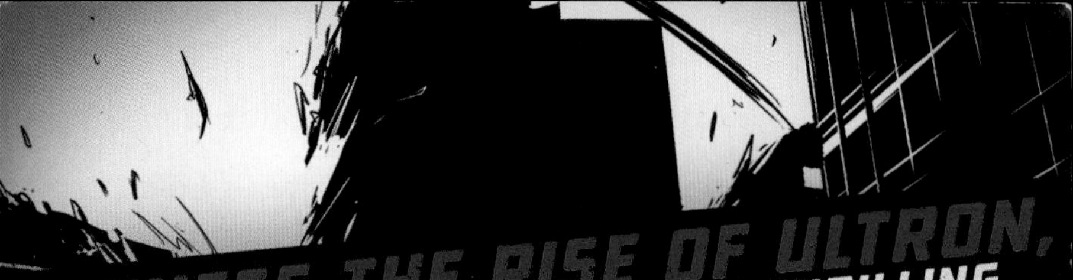

WITNESS THE RISE OF ULTRON, REIMAGINED AND RETOLD IN THRILLING SOUTH KOREAN MANHWA STYLE!

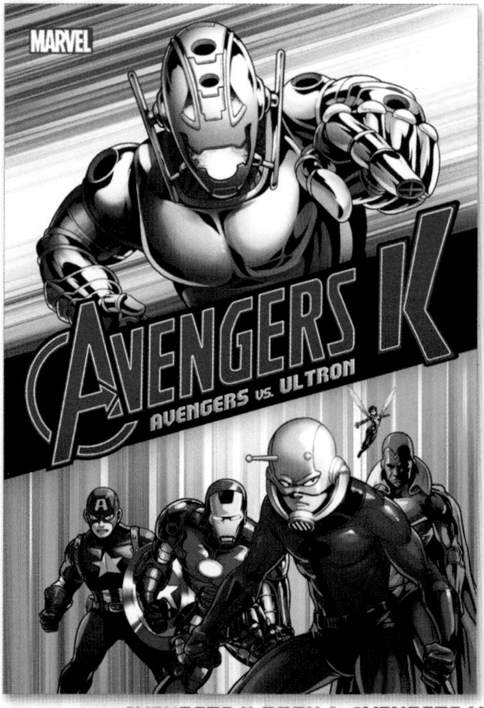
MARVEL
AVENGERS K
AVENGERS VS. ULTRON

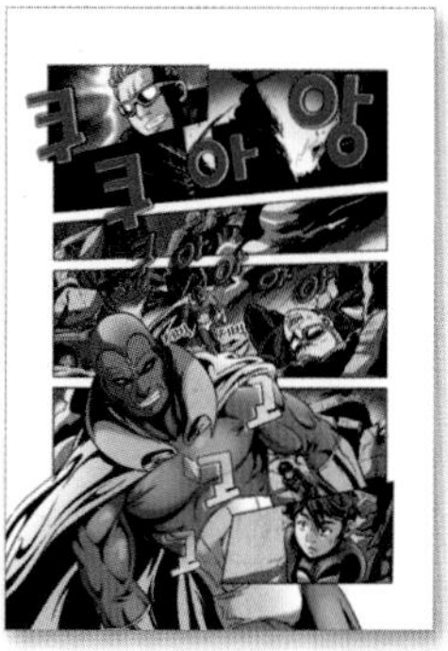

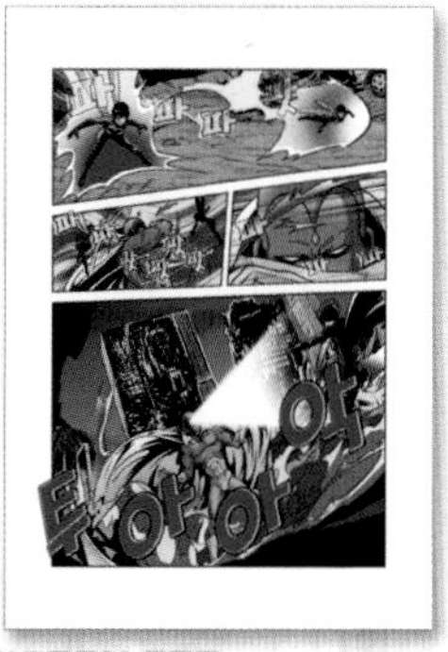

AVENGERS K BOOK 1: AVENGERS VS. ULTRON TPB
ISBN: 978-1-302-90120-2

COLLECTED IN ENGLISH FOR THE FIRST TIME!

AVAILABLE MAY 2016
IN PRINT AND DIGITAL WHEREVER BOOKS ARE SOLD

MARVEL